FAITH LESSONS

ON THE

early

CHURCH

CONQUERING THE GATES OF HELL

PARTICIPANT'S GUIDE

Also Available from Ray Vander Laan

Video and Group Resources

Faith Lessons on the Death and Resurrection of the Messiah
Faith Lessons on the Life and Ministry of the Messiah
Faith Lessons on the Promised Land
Faith Lessons on the Prophets and Kings of Israel

Book and Audiocassette

Echoes of His Presence

CD-Rom

Jesus: An Interactive Journey

FAITH LESSONS

ON THE

early

CHURCH

CONQUERING THE GATES OF HELL

PARTICIPANT'S GUIDE

Ray Vander Laan

with
Stephen and Amanda Sorenson

GRAND RAPIDS, MICHIGAN 49530

ZONDERVAN™

Faith Lessons on the Early Church Participant's Guide
Copyright © 2000 by Ray Vander Laan

Requests for information should be addressed to:

Zondervan, *Grand Rapids, Michigan 49530*

ISBN 0-310-67969-9

Interior design by Sherri Hoffman

Printed in the United States of America

04 05 06 /❖ DC/ 21 20 19 18 17 16 15 14 13 12 11

contents

introduction

Because God speaks to us through the Scriptures, studying them is a rewarding experience. The inspired human authors of the Bible, as well as those to whom the words were originally given, were Jews living in the Middle East. God's words and actions spoke to them with such power, clarity, and purpose that they wrote them down and carefully preserved them as an authoritative body of literature.

God's use of human servants in revealing Himself resulted in writings that clearly bear the stamp of time and place. The message of the Scriptures is, of course, eternal and unchanging—but the circumstances and conditions of the people of the Bible are unique to their times. Consequently, we most clearly understand God's truth when we know the cultural context within which He spoke and acted and the perception of the people with whom He communicated. This does not mean that God's revelation is unclear if we don't know the cultural context. Rather, by learning how to think and approach life as Abraham, Moses, Ruth, Esther, and Paul did, modern Christians will deepen their appreciation of God's Word. To fully apply the message of the Bible to our lives, we must enter the world of the Bible and familiarize ourselves with its culture.

That is the purpose of this study. The events and characters of the Bible will be presented in their original settings. Although the videos offer the latest archaeological research, this series is not intended to be a definitive cultural and geographical study of the lands of the Bible. No original scientific discoveries are revealed here. The purpose of this study is to help us better understand God's revealed mission for our lives by enabling us to hear and see His words in their original context.

understanding the world of the Bible

More than 3,800 years ago, God spoke to His servant Abraham: "Go, walk through the length and breadth of the land, for I am giving it to you" (Genesis 13:17). From the outset, God's choice of a Hebrew nomad to begin His plan of salvation (that is still unfolding) was linked to the selection of a specific land where His redemptive work would begin. The nature of God's covenant relationship with His people demanded a place where their faith could be exercised and displayed to all nations so that the world would know of *Yahweh*, the true and faithful God. God showed the same care in preparing a land for His chosen people as He did in preparing a people to live in that land. For us to fully understand God's plan and purpose for His people, we must first understand the nature of the place He selected for them.

In the Old Testament, God promised to protect and provide for the Hebrews. He began by giving them Canaan—a beautiful, fertile land where He would shower His blessings upon them. To possess this land, however, the Israelites had to live obediently before God. The Hebrew Scriptures repeatedly link Israel's obedience to God to the nation's continued possession of Canaan, just as they link its disobedience to the punishment of exile (Leviticus 18:24–28). When the Israelites were exiled from the Promised Land (2 Kings 18:11), they did not experience God's blessings. Only when they possessed the land did they know the fullness of God's promises.

By New Testament times, the Jewish people had been removed from the Promised Land by the Babylonians due to Israel's failure to live obediently before God (Jeremiah 25:4–11). The exile lasted seventy years, but its impact upon God's people was astounding. New patterns of worship developed, and scribes and experts in God's law shaped the new commitment to be faithful to Him. The prophets predicted the appearance of a Messiah like King David who would revive the kingdom of the Hebrew people.

But the Promised Land had become home to many other groups of people whose religious practices, moral values, and lifestyles conflicted with those of the Jews. Living as God's witnesses took on added difficulty as Greek, Roman, and Samaritan worldviews mingled with that of the Israelites. The Promised Land was divided between kings and governors, usually under the authority of one foreign empire or another. But the mission of God's people did not change. They were still to live so that *the world may know that our God is the true God.* And the land continued to provide them opportunity to encounter the world that desperately needed to know this reality.

The Promised Land was the arena within which God's people would serve Him faithfully as the world watched. The land God chose for His people was on the crossroads of the world. A major trade route, the Via Maris, ran through it. God intended for the Israelites to take control of the cities along this route and thereby exert influence on the nations around them. Through their righteous living, the Hebrews would reveal the one true God, *Yahweh*, to the world. They failed to accomplish this mission, however, because of their unfaithfulness.

The Jewish Gospel in a Greek world

From the beginning, God's plan was to reclaim His world. The Jewish people of the Bible had made God known to many of the nations of the world as people from those nations traveled through Israel. The Assyrian dispersion and the Babylonian exile spread God-fearing Jewish people around the known world. Many of them returned to Jerusalem for the yearly feasts that God had commanded. God had prepared carefully and well for the next stage in His great plan of salvation: His people must now live *so that the world may know* in all the world—not just in one small place.

If the arena had changed, the mission had not. The people of God would reveal Him to people in places such as Rome, Athens, and the cities of Roman provinces such as Syria and Macedonia. The most pagan of all provinces, Asia Minor, would become a stronghold for the followers of God and the Messiah Jesus. They would serve Him while the nations of the world watched and listened.

The triumph of the Christian faith is nowhere more striking or unexpected than in the Roman Province of Asia Minor. Known for immorality in lifestyle and in religious practice, this region became Christian within 150 years of Jesus' ministry in Israel. The early missionary, Paul (Shaul in Hebrew), spent a great deal of time here and wrote several letters to the followers of Jesus in this province. Peter wrote his letters to the believers here, and John wrote Revelation (and his letters) to the churches of this province. The effectiveness of the early believers is amazing and raises a host of questions with great implications for our world today. How did Jesus prepare His followers for such a mission? What empowered them? What kind of commitments did they have to make to their mission? What did they do that had such an impact on the people of Asia? Some answers to these questions become clear when we study the Biblical stories in the context in which they occurred.

pliny

One of the most important sources of information about life in Asia Minor at the time of the early church comes from a Roman governor named Pliny. His letters, written to the emperor Trajan (A.D. 98–117) are a fascinating description of the relationship between the early believers and the pagan Gentiles in the province of Asia Minor. Pliny's work provides helpful insights for understanding the stories and teachings of Scripture. In addition, Pliny provides many insights into the view of the new faith held by the people of his time who were not Christians.

Trajan had appointed Pliny to bring order to the area of Pontus (in Asia Minor) because of riots and unrest due to local corruption. Pliny proceeded to ban all social, political, and religious organizations, which created great suffering for the Christians because they were not considered one of the legal religions. Pliny noted that the "superstition" (Christianity) had spread throughout the province and left ancient temples deserted.

Pliny made it clear that being a Christian was a capital offense, and many were accused and charged. Pliny offered them several chances to renounce their faith and then they were executed. In one letter to Trajan, he asked what should be done to those who renounced their faith. Were they still criminals for their actions while they were members of the sect or was their rejection of Jesus sufficient? Trajan replied by making adherence to Christianity a capital offense, although the believers were not to be sought out.

our purpose

Biblical writers assumed that their readers were familiar with Middle Eastern geography. Today, unfortunately, many Christians do not have even a basic geographical knowledge of the region. This study is designed to help solve that problem. We will be studying the people and events of the Bible in their geographical and historical contexts. Once we know the who, what, and where of a Bible story, we will be able to understand the why. By deepening our understanding of God's Word, we will be able to strengthen our relationships with Him.

Western Christianity tends to spiritualize the faith of the people of the Bible. Modern Christians do not always do justice to God's desire that His people live faithfully for Him in specific places, influencing the cultures around them by their words and actions. Instead of seeing the places to which God called His people as crossroads from which to influence the world, we focus on the glorious destination to which we are traveling as we ignore the world around us. We are focused on the destination, not the journey. We have unconsciously separated our walk with God from our responsibility to the world in which He has placed us.

In one sense, our earthly experience is simply preparation for an eternity in the new "Promised Land." Preoccupation with this idea, however, distorts the mission God has set for us. That mission is the same one He gave to the Israelites: to live obediently *within* the world so that through us, *the world may know that our God is the one true God.*

everything to lose, nothing to gain

questions to think about

1. Take a minute to list what you find to be the most difficult places or situations in which to minister in the world around you.

2. What factors make it difficult to share your faith in these places or situations?

video notes

Galilee—Jesus the Rabbi Builds a Community of Followers

Caesarea Philippi—Jesus Asks the All-Important Question

The Mount of Olives—Jesus Delivers His Final Message

video highlights

1. Note the region of Asia Minor on the map of the Roman Empire on page 16. Which characteristics of this area made it a seemingly unlikely place for Jewish disciples from Galilee to evangelize?

2. In what specific ways did Jesus the rabbi, through His personal relationship with His disciples, prepare them for their future ministry?

3. Why was it so important for the disciples—as Peter did in Caesarea Philippi—to affirm who Jesus was?

4. Why was it so important for the disciples to actually see Jesus ascend to heaven?

The Roman Empire

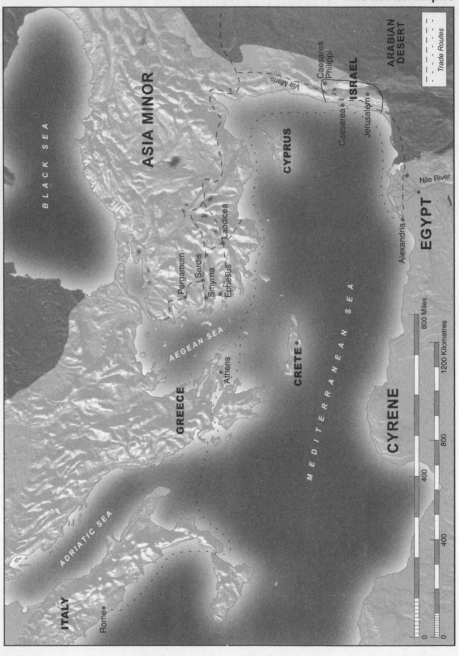

small group bible discovery

Topic A: Jesus the Rabbi

After learning the construction trade with Joseph, His earthly father, Jesus became a teacher—a rabbi. During Jesus' time, the term *rabbi* did not refer to a specific office or occupation. Rather, it was a term of respect, meaning "great one" or "my master." The students of a rabbi—*talmidim*—were passionately devoted to him. They watched and noted everything he said and did so that they could do the same. As the rabbi lived and interpreted the Torah, his disciples sought to imitate him. Their overriding passion was to become like him. Eventually, they also would become teachers, passing on what they'd learned to their *talmidim*.

Galilee of Jesus' Ministry

1. In which area of Israel did Jesus conduct His ministry and perform most of His miracles? What were the people there like? (See Matthew 4:13–16; 11:20–24.)

2. Each rabbi encouraged his disciples to take on the "yoke of Torah," to commit to obeying Torah as the rabbi interpreted and taught it. How did Jesus describe His "yoke," and how did it compare to the "yoke" of some other rabbis? (See Matthew 11:28–30; 23:1–4.)

3. To be a *talmid* meant far more than to learn what the rabbi knew. What do the following verses reveal about what Jesus wanted His disciples to be and do—how He wanted them to live out their faith in daily life?

Reference	What It Meant to Be Like the Rabbi
Matthew 28:16–20	
Mark 1:16–20	
Mark 3:13–19	

Luke 6:40	
Luke 9:1–6	
Luke 14:26–27	
John 8:31	
John 13:13–17	

THE TRUTH OF THE MATTER

The "Yoke" of the Kingdom of Heaven

Many Christians today recognize that salvation is a gift from God and so place little emphasis on "keeping the law" of the Bible. It is true that Jesus did away with "law keeping" by obeying the law completely and by offering salvation through grace to everyone who trusts in Him. Yet it is also true that Jesus did not suggest that obedience to the Word of God was any less important because of His completed work. In fact, He commanded His followers to "go and make disciples ... teaching them to *obey everything* I have commanded you" (Matthew 28:19–20, italics added).

If we are to be like Jesus—to be His disciples—we must desire to be like Him in all ways, which includes obeying Him as He obeys His Father. Just as obedience was vital to the first-century disciples who went to pagan regions and proclaimed God's way to live, obedience is vital to us today. If we are to impact our world for God, we must have the same commitment to the lifestyle God demands and Jesus exemplified.

PROFILE OF A MASTER

Jesus the Master Teacher

The great teachers (rabbis) during Jesus' day used a technique that was later called *remez*. In their teaching, they would use part of a Scripture passage in a discussion, assuming that their audience's knowledge of the Bible would allow them to deduce for themselves the fuller meaning of the teaching. Apparently Jesus, who possessed a brilliant understanding of Scripture and strong teaching skills, used this method often.

For example, when the children shouted "Hosanna" to Him in the temple and the chief priests and teachers of the law became indignant (Matthew 21:15), Jesus responded by quoting Psalm 8:2: "From the lips of children and infants you have ordained praise." The religious leaders' anger at Jesus can be better understood when we realize that the next phrase in the psalm reveals why children and infants offer praise—because the enemies of God would be silenced. The religious leaders realized that Jesus was implying that they were God's enemies.

Jesus used this teaching method again when speaking to Zacchaeus. "For the Son of Man came to seek and to save what was lost," Jesus said (Luke 19:10). The background to this statement is probably Ezekiel 34. God, angry with Israel's leaders for scattering and harming His flock, stated that He would become the shepherd and would seek the lost ones and save them. Based on this, the people of Jesus' day understood that the Messiah to come would "seek and save" the lost. By using this phrase, knowing that His listeners knew the Scripture, Jesus communicated several things. To the people, He communicated, "I am the Messiah and also God." To the religious leaders, whose influence kept Zacchaeus out of the crowd, He said, "You have scattered and harmed God's flock." To Zacchaeus, He said, "You are one of God's lost sheep, and He still loves you."

Jesus best fit the type of rabbi believed to have *s'mikhah*, the authority to make new interpretations of the Torah. Whereas most teachers of the law could only teach accepted interpretations, teachers with authority could make new interpretations and pass legal judgments. Crowds were amazed because Jesus taught with authority (Matthew 7:28–29), and some people questioned His authority (Matthew 21:23–27).

Topic B: Confronting the "Gates of Hades"

Jesus took His disciples from their familiar, Jewish religious sur-
roundings in Galilee to the equally religious, but pagan, city of Caesarea Philippi thirty miles away. Caesarea Philippi was a world center
of Pan worship, boasting a yearly Pan festival and an assortment of
other pagan shrines. Here Jesus gave them an essential lesson that
would prepare them for their future ministry in a pagan world.

1. Why was Peter's use of the word "living" so significant
    when he declared Jesus to be "the Christ, the Son of the
    living God"? (See Matthew 16:13–16.)

Artist's Rendering of Caesarea Philippi

2. Read Matthew 16:17–19.

    a. Given the setting in which this conversation took place, what did Jesus mean by "on this rock I will build my church"?

    b. Since the cave at the base of the cliff was called the "gates of Hades," what did Jesus mean when He said, "I will build my church, and the gates of Hades will not overcome it"?

3. Read Mark 8:34–9:1.

    a. What types of people were probably present when Jesus addressed the crowd near Caesarea Philippi?

DID YOU KNOW?

"The gates of Hades," a phrase found in Matthew 16:18, can be translated as "hell." Hades, called *Sheol* in the Old Testament Hebrew, is the place where departed spirits live. Apparently it was frequently used as a synonym for hell. (See Psalm 9:17; 55:15; 116:3.)

b. When Jesus invited the crowd to "come after" Him—
    to be His disciples, to be like Him—what did He tell
    them was required?

c. What would the term "deny" have meant to people
    who worshiped Pan and other false gods? (See also
    1 Peter 4:3–4 and 1 John 2:15–17.)

d. How did Jesus' strong words about being ashamed
    relate to how the disciples may have felt when Jesus
    confronted the pagan crowd? (See Mark 8:38.)

DATA FILE

Pagan Worship by the Cave in Caesarea Philippi

At the foot of one of the ridges of Mount Hermon in northern Israel stands a 100-foot cliff that for centuries held great significance to pagan worshipers. Here, an underground river (one of the fountainheads of the Jordan River) flowed from a large, deep cave named the Grotto of Pan. The cave was also known as the "gates of Hades" (hell) because pagan people believed that their gods used this cave to travel to and from the underworld.

The Grotto of Pan

As part of their fertility rituals, worshipers carved small niches on the cliff face to hold statues or idols of their gods. These included Pan and his sexual partners (nymphs) as well as other goddesses of fertility cults such as Nemesis from Phoenicia—the home of Asherah and Baal. Idols of Athena and Aphrodite have been unearthed at this site, and Baal may have been worshiped here as well.

Several hundred years before Jesus visited this area with His disciples, Greek soldiers of Alexander the Great built a shrine dedicated to Pan—the fertility god of mountains and forests—on the flat area in front of the cliff face. A thirty-by-forty-five-foot platform served as the sacred place for Pan. Nearby, a Pan statue stood in a vaulted, artificial cave that contained niches holding the statues of nymphs who supposedly had sexual relations with Pan.

In front of the cave, about 20 B.C., Herod the Great built a small, thirty-by-sixty-foot temple of white marble dedicated to emperor Augustus. During religious rites, animals were sacrificed and thrown into the cave. If the water rushing out contained blood, the gods had rejected the sacrifice.

This temple, which honored a human who called himself a god, greatly offended Jewish people who followed the Torah (such as the disciples).

Pagan God Niche

Near the cliff in which the cave was located, Herod the Great's son, Herod Phillip, built his capital city during Jesus' lifetime. He also enlarged the religious shrines. After Jesus' time, this location continued to be a focal point of pagan worship. A fifteen-by-forty-eight-foot Nemesis shrine, for example, was built to honor one of the nymphs of Pan—the goddess of revenge.

Emperor Trajan (A.D. 98–117) built a thirty-five-by-fifty-foot temple dedicated to Zeus in this same area. And, about A.D. 220, the forty-eight-by-sixty-foot Goat Shrine and the thirty-five-by-twenty-two-foot Court of the Dancing Goats were built. In both of these, worshipers feasted on sacrificed (possibly raw) meat, made sacrifices to Pan and other pagan deities, observed mating goats, and held religious celebrations. Sexual rituals (maybe even sexual relations between humans and goats) probably took place here as well. Nothing could have been more offensive to people who believed in God.

The Temple Podium

WORTH OBSERVING . . .

The Meaning of the "Rock"

Throughout church history, there has been discussion and debate on exactly what Jesus meant when He said, "on this rock I will build my church" (Matthew 16:18). As we've explored in this session, the cliff face in Caesarea Philippi that was used for centuries in idol worship provides yet another metaphor for the "rock" Jesus mentioned. In this setting, the "rock" can mean the "rock" of pagan values and dead idolatry that was so prominent in Caesarea Philippi. Jesus, then, was saying that His church would replace those values. Two other viewpoints within the traditional understanding of the meaning of the "rock" are:

1. The "rock" is the confession of Peter that Jesus is Christ (i.e., Christ, the Son of the living God, is the foundation of the church. See Acts 4:10–11 and 1 Corinthians 3:10–15).
2. The "rock" is Peter, whose confession on behalf of the other disciples acknowledged the truth that Jesus is Messiah.

Topic C: Jesus' Ascension

The ascension of Jesus to heaven, as the disciples watched on the Mount of Olives (Acts 1:9–12), was a key lesson in their preparation for future ministry. To the Jews, the ascension clearly declared God's ultimate victory over the world, including the defeat of Rome and paganism. But the ascension also conveyed a radical message to the Gentile world, one that would directly challenge emperor worship in Asia Minor.

1. Read Daniel's vision, found in Daniel 7:13–14. How did Jesus' ascension relate to this prophecy?

The Districts of Jerusalem

A David's City
B New City
C Upper City
D Business District
E Temple Mount
F Lower City
G Herod's Palace

1 Eastern Gate
2 Southern Stairs
3 Royal Stoa
4 Robinson's Arch
5 Wilson's Arch
6 Tyropoeon Street
7 Warren's Gate
8 Antonia
9 Tadi Gate
10 Pool of Bethesada
11 First Wall
12 Second Wall
13 Garden Gate
14 Towers (Damascus) Gate
15 Golgotha (?)
16 Garden Tomb
17 Spring of Gihon
18 Hinnom Valley
19 Theatre
20 Citadel and Herod's Palace
21 Essene Quarter
22 Mansions
23 Mount of Olives
24 Kidron Valley
25 Huldah Gates

2. As religious Jewish men, the disciples would have known about Daniel's vision of the Messiah and the coming of God's kingdom. Note the similarities between Daniel's vision (Daniel 7:13–14) and Jesus' last teachings and His ascension as recorded in the following passages. Also note the impact these events had on the disciples.

Passage	Similarities	Impact on Disciples
Matthew 28:16–20		
Luke 24:50–53		
Acts 1:6–11		

3. What did Jesus tell His disciples just before He ascended? (See Matthew 28:16–20 and Acts 1:3–9.)

4. What did the disciples witness firsthand, and how would news of this event be received by the Roman world?

Topic D: The Power of *Talmidim*

Jesus calls His followers to be *talmidim* who make *talmidim*. This means His disciples are to seek to be like Him. They are to develop relationships with other people who imitate them as they imitate Jesus. One reason the gospel spread so rapidly during the time of the early church was because Jesus' disciples had a passion to be like Jesus and put into practice what they had been taught by Jesus or by other Christians. Notice how Jesus prepared His *talmidim* and how they responded.

1. Instruction and practice are an important part of any training effort. During His ministry on earth, Jesus sent disciples out into the world to minister to others on at least two occasions. In each instance note His instructions, what the disciples did, and the result.

    a. The Twelve (see Luke 9:1–6).

    b. The seventy-two (see Luke 10:1–12, 17–20).

2. In Matthew 28:16–20, Jesus gave His disciples their instructions. Note the way in which they carried them out.

    a. Acts 26:19–29

b. 1 Corinthians 4:15–17

c. 1 Thessalonians 1:6–7

d. Hebrews 6:12; 13:7

WORTH OBSERVING . . .

The Relationship That Can Change the World

Jesus' disciples, the ones He called into relationship with Him as *talmidim*, made such an impact on the province of Asia Minor—the most pagan of all the Roman provinces—that it became the most Christian province in the Roman Empire. Jesus desires the same kind of relationship with His disciples today. To have that kind of relationship in our world means that we must:

- Know God's Word and Jesus' interpretation of it.
- Be passionate in our devotion to that Word and Jesus' example.
- Follow Him even if we are not sure of the final destination.
- Live by His teaching, which means we must know that teaching well.
- Be obsessed with being like Him as much as is humanly possible.
- Develop meaningful relationships with others so that they will observe us and seek to imitate our love, devotion to God, and our Jesus-like lifestyle. (See 1 Corinthians 2:16; 11:1; Galatians 3:26–27.)

By God's grace, people with totally committed relationships to Christ can change the most pagan culture—including our own.

DATA FILE

The Amazing Galileans

Jesus focused His ministry in one small place in Israel: Galilee, in the three cities of Korazin, Capernaum, and Bethsaida. Although many people today assume that Galileans were simple, uneducated peasants who lived in an isolated area, the truth is they interacted more with the world than the Jews of Jerusalem. After all, the Via Maris trade route passed through Galilee, exposing them to many different peoples and cultures.

The Galileans were also the most religious Jews in the world during Jesus' time. They revered and knew the Scriptures well. They were passionately committed to living out their faith and passing their faith, knowledge, and lifestyle on to their children. This led to the establishment of vibrant religious communities; a strong commitment to families and country; and active participation in the local synagogues—the community centers of that day. In fact, more famous Jewish teachers came from Galilee than from anywhere else.

The Galileans resisted the pagan influences of Hellenism far longer than their Judean counterparts, and when the great revolt against the Romans and their collaborators finally occurred (A.D. 66–74), it began among the Galileans.

Clearly God carefully prepared the environment in which Jesus was born and reared so that He would have exactly the context He needed in order to present His message of *malchut Shemayim*—the kingdom of heaven—effectively, and so that people would understand and join His new movement.

A deeper knowledge of Galilee and its people helps us understand the great faith and courage of His disciples, who left Galilee and shared the good news with the world. (Evidence indicates that Judas Iscariot was apparently the only non-Galilean among Jesus' twelve, closest disciples.) The disciples' courage, the message they taught, the methods they used, and their complete devotion to God and His Word were born in Galilee's religious communities.

Topic E: Idolatry in Northern Israel

Although God gave the tribe of Dan a designated territory in the Shep-helah between the coastal plain and the mountains of Judea, they did not capture this land in the name of the Lord. Instead, they packed up their families and settled near the northern border of Israel in an area that was widely known as a pagan worship center.

1. What did the Danites do when they discovered that a house in this region had a Levite priest as well as an idol, carved image, and other articles of pagan worship? (See Judges 18:1–2, 11–20.)

2. How did the Danites go about establishing their home-land? (See Judges 18:27–31.)

3. After Solomon's death, the nation of Israel split into two kingdoms—Israel in the north and Judah in the south. What did Jeroboam, king of Israel, do to preserve his king-dom? (See 1 Kings 12:26–32.)

4. What happened in Israel as a result of what King Jeroboam did in Dan? (See 1 Kings 16:15–19, 23–26, 29–33.)

5. When God sent pagan nations to punish His people for their idol worship, what happened to the city of Dan? (See 1 Kings 15:18–20.)

faith Lesson

Time for Reflection

Read the following passage of Scripture and take the next few minutes to consider the ways in which Jesus prepared His disciples to fulfill the mission He had for them.

> Then the eleven disciples went to Galilee, to the mountain where Jesus had told them to go. When they saw him, they worshiped him; but some doubted. Then Jesus came to them and said, "All authority in heaven and on earth has been given to me. Therefore go and make disciples of all nations, baptizing them in the name of the Father and of the Son and of the Holy Spirit, and teaching them to obey everything I have commanded you. And surely I am with you always, to the very end of the age."

MATTHEW 28:16–20

These words, spoken by Jesus shortly before His ascension, conveyed a powerful and compelling message to His disciples. Jesus sent them out with "all authority." He clearly told them to teach obedience and "make disciples of all nations." And He promised to be with them always. Take some time to prayerfully consider not only what these words meant to the disciples who had lived as *talmidim* of Jesus the rabbi, but what they mean to you as you go out into your world.

Action Points

Take a moment to jot down an action step (or steps) that you will commit to this week as a result of what you have learned.

1. *As a rabbi, Jesus prepared His chosen disciples—His talmidim—to carry on His message after He was gone.* He lived in community with them, interpreting and modeling the Torah so that they would know how to live God's way. He taught them about His faith, which is a passionate commitment to act in accordance with what they believed.

   In what ways are you, or are you not, a true disciple of Jesus?

   As a disciple—a *talmid*—of Jesus, what are you willing to do this week in order to model Christ's love to an unbeliever?

2. *Shortly before going to Jerusalem for the last time, Jesus took His disciples to Caesarea Philippi, a pagan worship center. Here, His disciples realized anew that He was the Messiah, the Son of the living God.* He also assured them that His church would triumph—even over the gates of Hades (hell). How important this truth would become when the disciples faced personal suffering, even martyrdom, because of their commitment to Him.

Identify the "dead" gods and pagan values of our culture that need to be challenged and replaced with God's values.

Today, through the power of the living God, we can share our faith even in the most difficult situations. We can overcome the "gates of hell" in our culture. In what specific way(s) can you effectively influence your culture by seeking to be like Jesus?

3. *As eyewitnesses of His ascension, the disciples were empowered to boldly proclaim the message of Jesus to their world.* For His last teaching, Jesus took His disciples to the Mount of Olives and reminded them that they were His witnesses to the world. Then, before their eyes, He ascended into heaven. This dramatic scene inspired them to go out and tell everyone about the living Messiah who will one day return to claim His own.

Jesus' ascension greatly increased the faith of His disciples before they went out to fulfill their ministry in many nations. What difference does His ascension make to your faith?

Is Jesus' ascension so real to you that you are willing to take the "heat" and proclaim the *living* Christ no matter what? In what ways does it empower you to face the "Asia Minors" in your culture with confidence and power?

The salt of the earth

Questions to Think About

1. Describe the areas or ways in which you find it easy to compromise your faith and fit in with secular culture. What makes it difficult to stand up for Christ in these situations?

2. Describe the type of involvement in the secular world and with secular people that you as a Christian must have in order to communicate the message of Jesus to your culture.

3. Many of us have known Christians who seemed to be doing all the "right" spiritual things, yet compromised in one area and destroyed their testimony for God. What can we do to prevent such spiritual defeats?

video notes

John's Warning

The History of Sardis

Standing for God in a Pagan Culture

 The Shops

 The Synagogue

 The Church

The Salt of the Earth

video Highlights

1. What metaphor did John use to communicate his message
   to the church at Sardis? What was his message?

Christian Church in the Temple of Artemis

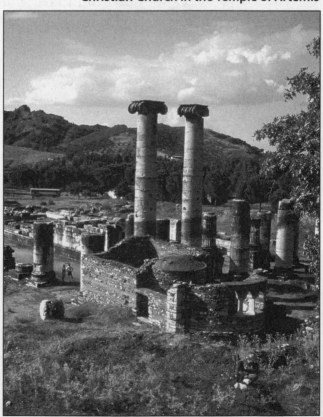

2. What do the archaeological discoveries presented in this video tell you about the worldview of the religious Jews and Christians in Sardis?

    a. Which of these discoveries most surprised you? Why?

3. Which aspects of this video connected with you as you thought about your life and your culture? Why?

PROFILE OF A CITY

Sardis

- Stood in the middle of the Hermus River Valley, just over fifty miles east of the Mediterranean Sea in what's now the country of Turkey. The main east-west trade route came through this valley.

- On a spur of Mount Tmolus, on the north side of the Hermus River Valley, the Lydians—dominant people in the interior of Asia from about 1000–550 B.C.—built the acropolis of Sardis.

- The capital of the Lydians, Sardis enjoyed half a millennium of artistic, architectural, and economic prosperity. Its most famous king, Croesus, became rich because his subjects discovered a way to pan gold from a nearby river using sheep fleeces that trapped flecks of gold.

- When Nebuchadnezzar conquered Assyria, Sardis became part of his empire. In 586 B.C., he conquered Judah, destroyed Jerusalem and the temple, and exiled many Jews. Apparently many of them were brought to Sardis, and out of this community of Jews the church of Sardis was later born. It is amazing to see how God prepared things ahead of time for His purpose.

- The Persians made Sardis their western capital, so it remained an important city. Alexander the Great ended the Persian Empire in 334 B.C., and Sardis became part of the Greek world.

Sardis Trade Routes

small Group Bible Discovery

Topic A: "Be Salt"

On more than one occasion, Jesus told His followers that they were to be "salt" wherever they went. He also cautioned them not to lose their "saltiness." Let's investigate what this metaphor means to the Christian walk.

1. Where did Jesus want His disciples to demonstrate their faith? What did He want them to be? (See Matthew 5:13; Mark 16:15.)

2. After seeing this video, describe in your own words what being the salt of the earth means.

3. Jesus knew that being the salt of the earth would be a challenge. Note how He prays for His disciples in John 17:15–18.

   a. What did Jesus ask for on behalf of His disciples as they lived out their faith in a pagan world? (See verse 15.)

b. Which phrase did Jesus use to describe His disciples in verse 16? What do you think this means?

c. To what did Jesus compare the disciples' ministry? (See verse 18.)

DID YOU KNOW?

Salt was very valuable during Jesus' day. It aided in the preservation of meat and enhanced the taste of food. But another less commonly known use of salt plays a key role in our understanding of what it means to be "salt" in our world.

During the first century, the people of Galilee used dome-shaped ovens made of hardened mud. Salt was mixed with dried dung—a common fuel—because the chemical reaction made the dung burn hotter and longer. Over time, however, the salt lost the qualities that made it effective. So, when it was no longer fit even for being mixed with manure, the "saltless" salt was thrown out.

Galilean Oven

As believers, God calls us to "mix" with sinful people and yet keep our distinctive Christian identity. God sent His disciples into an evil world to live out the good news. They were not to lose their faith by absorbing the values of the pagan world, nor were they to be isolated from unbelievers.

4. Read Matthew 5:13, Mark 9:50, and Luke14:34–35. What thought is expressed in all three of these passages?

    a. What can believers do to guard against losing their "saltiness"?

Topic B: John's Warning to the Church in Sardis

The history and archaeological discoveries made in Sardis provide valuable insights into the meaning and significance of the apostle John's warning to the church in that city.

1. Read Revelation 3:1–6 and answer the following questions, adding the appropriate historical or archaeological evidence.

    a. What paradox existed concerning the church in Sardis? (See verse 1.)

    b. What did John tell the Christians of Sardis to do? (See verse 2.)

c. Which specific steps toward reconciliation with God did John mention? (See verse 3.)

d. Which consequences did John say would be forthcoming if they did not change their ways? (See verse 3.)

e. According to verses 4–5, what do we learn about some of the Christians in Sardis? What hope did John promise to them and to others like them?

WORTH OBSERVING...

An Unlearned Lesson

About 550 B.C., the Persians captured the acropolis of Sardis after a Persian soldier named Lagoras saw a soldier from Sardis climb down a steep, hidden trail to retrieve his helmet. Amazingly, a similar situation occurred in about 200 B.C.! A Greek soldier named Hyroeades watched a soldier of Sardis throw garbage off the top and noticed that vultures would wait on the wall until the garbage was thrown again. So, the Greeks realized that that portion of the wall was unguarded and captured the city by attacking that spot at night.

Topic C: God's Strategy for the Early Missionaries

God has always intended for His people to live in the midst of culture and to influence it for Him. As they began to share the good news of Jesus with the world, the early missionaries went out from their home synagogues—the community center for Jewish life—and into the synagogues and cities of Asia Minor.

1. What was the "mission" of the Old Testament followers of God? (Read 1 Samuel 17:45–47; Isaiah 43:10–12.)

Roman Empire/Asia Minor

2. What was the mission of the early Christian missionaries? (See Acts 1:8; 10:37–43.)

3. Where had Jesus often taught His disciples, and what is significant about these locations? (Read Matthew 13:54; Mark 14:49.)

4. Read the following accounts of early Christian missionary efforts and note the strategy used.

Biblical Account	The Missionary Strategy
Acts 9:17–20	
Acts 13:1–5	
Acts 13:13–16	
Acts 14:1	
Acts 17:1–4	

DID YOU KNOW?

God Prepared Sardis to Receive the Good News

Jesus commanded His followers to "go into all the world and preach the good news to all creation" (Mark 16:15; Acts 1:8). It took His followers a while to understand the good news and what *all* the world meant, but as the Holy Spirit opened their hearts and minds, they began to go. Was the world prepared for them and their life-changing message? The answer is a resounding *yes*!

God had a specific strategy in mind for sending His message of salvation to the world. In Romans 1:16, Paul summarized it this way: "I am not ashamed of the gospel, because it is the power of God for the salvation of everyone who believes: *first* for the Jew, then for the Gentile [italics added]."

God commanded His people to reach the Jews first. Why? Because they were expecting the Messiah and were prepared to understand the gospel message because it involved the fulfillment of the Old Testament, which they knew. Also, God may have wanted Jews in each community to help Gentiles understand the roots of their newfound faith. So, when Paul, Silas, Barnabas, and other believers traveled to a new location, they went to the local synagogue and preached the news of Jesus Christ there. (See Acts 9:20; 13:5, 14; 14:1; 17:1–2, 10–12; 18:1–7, 19; 19:8.)

Although we don't know who started the church in Sardis, Jews were already living there when the early missionaries arrived with the gospel. In fact, hundreds of years before Jesus came to earth, God used pagan rulers to scatter Jewish populations across Asia Minor. For example, it is likely that Nebuchadnezzar of Babylon exiled Jews to Sardis when he destroyed Jerusalem in 586 B.C. Later, Cyrus of Persia encouraged more Jews to move to Asia Minor, and Antiochus—the pagan Greek king—brought two thousand Jewish families to Asia Minor during the third century, B.C.

Some of the descendants of these Jews were in Jerusalem during Pentecost (Acts 2:9), while others lived in cities such as Sardis—a key, influential city at the crossroads of the world. The Jewish presence in Asia Minor dramatically increased the impact and spread of the gospel. Truly

God is in control of all things. All things work toward His plan (Romans 8:28), and God can use evil for good (see Genesis 50:20).

Today, God still does "advance" planning! Often He prepares the hearts of unbelievers so they'll be open to receiving the message of the Messiah. What's important is that we will be faithful to God's call and depend on Him to bring the spiritual fruit.

Topic D: A God-Centered Versus a Human-Centered Worldview

As the early Christian missionaries began spreading Jesus' message, they encountered views of the world and of the nature of truth that differed greatly from their own. The conflict between a God-centered view of the world and a human-centered view of the world remains to this day—as it has since the Garden of Eden. Will people acknowledge God as the supreme being over all, or will they act as if they are the ultimate? Do human beings determine truth, or is God the source of all truth?

1. Who does the Bible teach is the ultimate, sovereign authority in the universe? (See Psalm 22:27–29; Isaiah 29:13–16; Romans 9:20–21.)

2. What was the underlying issue in Satan's tempting offer to Eve? (See Genesis 3:1–7.)

3. Hellenism, the dominant worldview in the first century, viewed human beings as ultimate in the universe, the human mind the source of the greatest wisdom, right and wrong a human choice, human accomplishment the goal of life, and the human body the greatest beauty. How does this worldview contrast with what Paul wrote concerning the Christian worldview? (See 1 Corinthians 1:18–25.)

4. Whose sovereignty did the believers declare to their world, and how did Satan respond? (See Acts 17:22–24; Jude 4–8.)

5. What happens when people consider something or some-one other than God to be the ultimate authority? (See Romans 1:18–32.)

A STUDY IN CONTRASTS

Hellenism, the dominant worldview in the first century, stands in stark contrast to the truths of God found in the Bible.

Hellenism	The Biblical Perspective
Human beings are the image of gods.	Only God is God, He is the Lord of the universe, the Creator of mankind.
The human mind is the greatest source of wisdom.	God is the ultimate source of all wisdom.
Human beings determine truth—what is right and wrong.	God, the source of truth, has given us the standards that determine what's right and wrong.
Human accomplishment is the goal of life.	The goal of life is to glorify and serve God.
The human body and what human beings create is the highest standard of beauty.	Human beings create beauty because they are made in the image of God.

DID YOU KNOW?

Jewish synagogues were more than just places to worship. They served as community centers for Jewish life. In the synagogue, the Jews prayed, taught school, held legal court, celebrated special times, and even lodged travelers. This may help us to understand why the synagogue in Sardis was located in the pagan gymnasium—the center of Jewish teaching was placed within the center of Hellenistic teaching.

Synagogue in Sardis

DATA FILE

The Greek Gymnasium

Every major Hellenistic city had an educational institution called a gymnasium, in which citizens of the Greek/Roman community were taught the wisdom of Hellenism. Religious Jews during biblical times believed the gymnasium to be an abomination because education there was based on the view that humans are the ultimate source of truth, many activities were done naked, and students had to make certain pagan religious commitments in order to participate.

Gymnasium of Sardis

Several passages in Paul's writings imply that he was aware of gymnasiums: 1 Timothy 4:8 includes the expression "physical training" that is based on the Greek word for *gymnasium*; 1 Corinthians 9:24–27 mentions competitions such as boxing and running; and Galatians 2:2; 5:7 and Philippians 2:16 mention running. In Galatians 3:24, Paul also used the Greek word *paidagogos,* which referred to the slave attendant who accompanied students from wealthy families to school in order to tutor them in the lessons they received from the teacher in the gymnasium.

Features of the Gymnasium at Sardis

The Palaestra

In this large (six hundred by one hundred fifty feet), open area to the east of the Marble Court, physical education was done on the sand floor. Smaller rooms around the outside were also used for physical training— conditioning (weights and calisthenics), skill development (discus, javelin, jumping), and cardiovascular training (running). Also in these rooms the students relaxed with massage and oil treatments after their exercise and classroom learning.

The Didaskelion

Located on the outside of the open area, this school for academics provided rooms in which students learned and recited lessons. There were three levels of education: elementary (boys and girls ages five to twelve who studied reading and writing); secondary (boys and girls ages twelve to sixteen who studied philosophy, math, science, and music); and advanced (boys ages sixteen through adulthood who studied philosophy, medicine, music and science).

The Marble Court

This three-story, colonnaded courtyard was dedicated to the cult of the Roman emperor—believed to be the guardian of the truth being taught and exemplified in his life. All learning was devoted to him. Many niches in the walls served as pediments for statues. In the main apse was a statue of the emperor, who was honored with sacrifices and ceremonies during the educational process.

The Bath Complex

In the western section was the largest pool, the heated caldarium. East of this was a large, central hall and the warm pool (tepidarium). A nearby oblong hall held the cold pool (frigidarium) where students completed their bathing. There were also fountains in niches in the walls.

The Synagogue

Synagogue in the Gymnasium

Holding more than one thousand people (estimated), this is the largest synagogue ever found in the ancient world. It was not part of the original gymnasium and was added later, just after the time of the New Testament. Here, impressive mosaic floors added to the beauty of the structure and testify to the community's wealth. More than eighty inscriptions have been found in the synagogue that indicate that some Jews had significant status and wealth in Sardis and that others were Gentile converts.

Topic E: Standing for God in a Pagan World

Standing for God within an evil culture is something every individual follower of Christ is called to do. By studying what other followers of God have done to display their faith, we can learn more about displaying our faith to our world.

1. How did God describe the nature of pagan worship among Israel's neighbors during Old Testament times? (See Exodus 34:15–16.)

2. How did Paul describe the pagan world of his day, which would have included the city of Sardis? (See Romans 1:18–26.)

3. Where did Jesus intend for His followers to live out their faith? What did He desire for them? (See John 17:15–19.)

4. Where was Paul committed to proclaim his faith? What freedom did he claim? (See 1 Corinthians 9:19–23.)

5. What "freedom" did Christians who had lived pagan lifestyles not have? (Read 1 Corinthians 5:9–11.)

faith Lesson

Time for Reflection

Read the following passage of Scripture and take the next few minutes to consider the ways in which you can be "salt" in your world.

> But you are a chosen people, a royal priesthood, a holy nation, a people belonging to God, that you may declare the praises of him who called you out of darkness into his wonderful light. Once you were not a people, but now you are the people of God; once you had not received mercy, but now you have received mercy.
>
> Dear friends, I urge you, as aliens and strangers in the world, to abstain from sinful desires, which war against your soul. Live such good lives among the pagans that, though they accuse you of doing wrong, they may see your good deeds and glorify God on the day he visits us.
>
> 1 Peter 2:9–12

Consider the ways in which Peter's words:

- stand in contrast to the pagan worldview
- remind believers that they are to be in the world but not of it
- encourage obedience to God's commands
- reinforce the concept that they are God's witnesses to a pagan world.

Imagine that Peter wrote these words directly to you:

- In what ways can you declare God's praises?
- What are the sinful desires that wage war against your soul?

- In which aspects of life are you so committed to God's worldview that you seem to be a stranger in the world?
- In what ways can you live such a good life that people who do not know God take notice and glorify God?

Action Points

Take a moment to jot down an action step (or steps) that you will commit to this week as a result of what you have learned.

1. *Jesus sent His disciples out to be "salt" in an evil world.* They were to go into the world and live out the good news without compromise. They were to retain their distinctiveness without isolating themselves from unbelievers.

   The evidence of Sardis raises the question of whether the Jews and Christians of that city were a distinctive influence among their pagan neighbors or whether they compromised their calling and lost the distinctive beliefs and lifestyle that are essential to faith in God.

   Consider the ways in which you are being "salt" in the world and consider also the ways in which you may be avoiding the world and therefore are missing opportunities to share Jesus' message. Write down specific examples of both.

I am "salt" in an evil world:	I am avoiding the world:

As you consider the world in which you live, where in your community do you need to step out of your comfort zone and be "salt"?

2. *John used a well-known, local, historical metaphor when he warned the Christians of Sardis to influence their world without compromising with it.* "I know your deeds," he wrote, "you have a reputation of being alive, but you are dead. Wake up! . . . but if you do not wake up, I will come like a thief, and you will not know at what time I will come to you" (Revelation 3:1–3).

This reminder applies to Christians today as well. We must be careful to stay watchful, alert, and alive to what's going on in our Christian walk. Otherwise, we might become apathetic or make a mistake that would cause our witness to a watching world to collapse.

In what way(s) have you—even in small ways—compromised your faith? Note particularly the ways in which you have become careless or apathetic toward your Christian calling.

Which particular sin(s) do you need to repent of in order to straighten out your relationship with God? Be specific.

3. *Worldview is important.* The Greeks in Sardis taught Hellenism, which glorified human beings and considered them to be the center of the universe, the source of all wisdom. This view stands in opposition to the biblical worldview that recognizes God as Lord of the universe and the source of all truth.

The great spiritual struggle throughout human history has been whether or not people choose to recognize God as the supreme being or insist on declaring themselves as the ultimate being.

In what ways are you tempted to adopt a more human-centered worldview? Be specific.

I, _____, realize that my commitment to recognize God as Lord of the universe and as the supreme authority in my life needs to be strengthened. I want God to be at the center of my universe. In order to have a more God-centered worldview, I will _____

_____

_____.

SESSION THREE

where satan lives

Pergu
divnesis
Zeus
Zemula

if you got drunk
enough, you became no

questions to think about
c Dimenes

Oscalopus — god of healing — symbol
of the snake

1. What are some of the ways in which people today try to find meaning and significance on their own, without God?

2. In what ways do people—even Christians—take credit for things that God has done? List subtle as well as obvious ways.

3. When you are trying to follow God but people around you are pursuing other directions, what enables you to persevere in your faith even when the pressure mounts to go along with others?

video notes

The City of Pergamum—Where Satan Has His Throne

The Temples of Counterfeit Gods

Dionysus

Asclepius

Demeter

Others

The True Source of Meaning in Life

video highlights

1. Were you surprised to discover the ways in which Satan "counterfeited" the claims of Jesus in Pergamum? Why or why not?

2. How would you define what John meant by "Satan's throne" and the place "where Satan lives"?

3. What parallels do you see between the worship of the various gods of Pergamum and our own culture? In what ways can these activities and beliefs in our culture be identified as the place "where Satan lives"?

4. Describe what you think it was like to live as a Christian in Pergamum.

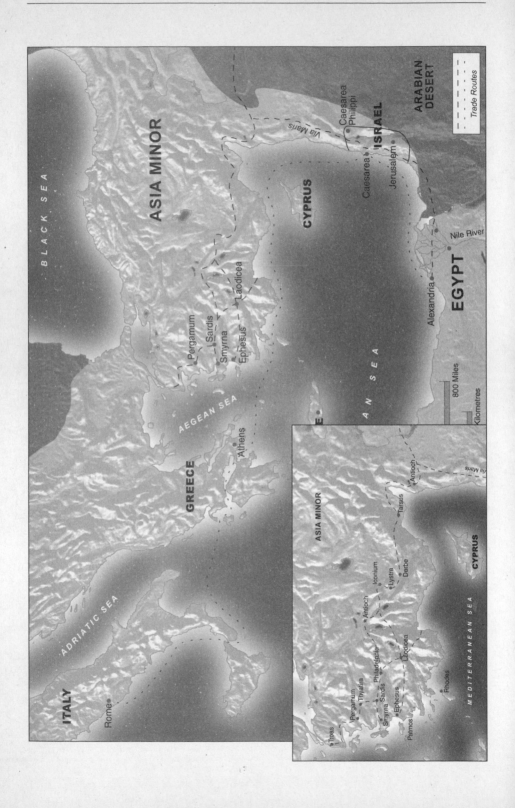

PROFILE OF A CITY

Pergamum

Pergamum (now Bergama) is located in the northern part of the Roman province of Asia Minor, along the Caicus River about ten miles from the Aegean Sea. From the third century B.C. until well into the fourth century A.D., its kings controlled a major trade road from the East (Persia) to the Mediterranean world.

Following the city's conquest by Alexander the Great in 334 B.C., its strategic location was recognized by Lysimachos, who turned it into a military base. From that point on, it became an increasingly significant Hellenistic city—rich in culture, spectacular in architecture, and powerful in its worship of pagan gods.

Its last king, Attalos III, willed the city to the Roman Empire so that its glory would not be spoiled by war. This proved to be a wise move because the Romans respected its cultural glory and religious character, making Pergamum the capital of the province of Asia Minor for a period of time. The Romans also left their mark on the city when it became the first city in which the cult of "divine" Caesars was established.

Pergamum

small Group Bible Discovery

Topic A: The Struggle Between God and Satan (Evil)

Since before the human race was created, a great battle has taken place between God and Satan. The early Christians realized that the gods of their pagan neighbors were, in fact, counterfeits of Satan designed to deceive them and lure them away from following God.

1. What basic conflict is described throughout the Bible? (See Genesis 3:1–15; Revelation 12:7–11.)

2. During His ministry on earth, what did Jesus demonstrate and accomplish related to the battle between God and Satan? (See Matthew 8:28–32; 12:22–28; Mark 1:21–27; Hebrews 2:14–15.)

3. What role in this battle did Jesus assign to His disciples, and in what way(s) did He encourage them? (See Matthew 10:1, 7–8; Luke 10:17–20.)

4. What is Satan's nature and what does he try to accomplish? (See Genesis 3:1–5; Matthew 4:1–4; John 8:44; 2 Corinthians 11:13–14.)

5. In contrast to what Satan wants people to think, who is really in charge of this world? (See Ephesians 1:18–23; 1 Timothy 6:13–16.)

THE TRUTH OF THE MATTER:

Giving God the Honor He Is Due

Satan has always wanted to rob God of the credit and honor due to Him. Because the deified emperors and gods of Pergamum such as Asclepius, Demeter, Dionysus, and Zeus received credit and honor that was due to God alone, they were demonic counterfeits. Things haven't changed much in our world today. Satan still wants people to believe that we have the authority to decide what's ours, what's right and wrong, and so on.

Our culture has bought into Satan's lie. People today (most Christians included) act as if credit is due the hard worker, the educated and successful people, people who care for their physical bodies properly, etc. But this perspective denies that God alone is Lord and provides everything we need—food, health, joy, wealth, etc. As the pagan cults of Pergamum illustrate, there is no place for God when we assume that perspective. *Anyone who fails to give God the credit He deserves is where Satan lives! Satan rules where people take credit for things due God, or give His honor to others.*

If Christians are to be faithful witnesses to the Lord of Lords and King of Kings, we must choose a different perspective. We must give Him credit and honor for *all* that He has provided and done for us. God is Lord of all and must be praised for all!

Topic B: Jesus Prepared His Disciples

Satan is diabolically clever and has deceived people from the beginning of human history. It is remarkable how closely the ancient pagan religions imitated and claimed to provide the same blessings that God provides. Knowing what His followers would encounter in pagan cities such as Pergamum, Jesus prepared them well to refute Satan's claims. Notice how He prepared them to deal with each of the claims below.

Dionysus

1. The priests of Dionysus claimed that their god could turn water into wine, but it was done in his temple in secret. (See John 2:1–11.)

2. Demeter, the goddess of grain, supposedly provided daily food for people. (See Matthew 4:4; 14:19; John 6:1–14.)

3. The followers of Demeter believed that she offered them the possibility of resurrection and forgiveness of sins through ceremonial washing in bulls' blood. (See John 11:17–26, 38–44; 20:26–30; 1 Corinthians 15:3–8; Hebrews 9:11–14.)

Asclepius

Asclepius

4. Asclepius was known as the god of healing and received honor from those who had been healed. (See John 5:1–13.)

5. Zeus, whose temple could be seen from a great distance, claimed to be the giver of life, lord of all, and creator of all. (See John 1:1–3; 10:10; 11:25–26, 41–44; Revelation 17:14.)

6. The Roman emperor, who declared himself to be the son of a god, lord of all, and the source of truth, demanded to be worshiped as god. (See John 1:10–11; 12:27–33; Acts 1:4–11.)

DATA FILE

Clever Counterfeits: The False Claims of the Cults

Each of the cults in Pergamum was a counterfeit, a clever copy of things that God alone provides. Each god took credit or honor away from God, thus giving it to something human or of human invention.

False Gods	False Claim(s)	The Truth
Zeus	Acclaimed as king of kings, lord of lords, creator of the universe.	God alone is King of Kings, Lord of Lords, Creator of the universe.
Dionysus	Reputed to provide joy, eternal life, and meaning; said to be able to change water into wine.	God alone provides these through Jesus, who turned water into wine and rose from the dead.
Demeter	Said to provide daily bread, resurrection, and eternal life through the blood of animals.	God alone provides these through Jesus, who fed thousands of people miraculously and shed His blood and rose from the dead so that people might receive eternal life.
Asclepius	Reputed to provide good health, healing from disease, and eternal life.	God alone provides these through Jesus, who healed many people, rose from the dead, and provides eternal life.
Emperor Worship	Emperor was viewed as lord of all, the supreme source of truth in the universe.	Jesus, seated at God's right hand, is Lord of Lords and King of the universe; God is the source of all truth.
People Today	Give themselves or other things credit for what God has really done (healing, etc.).	People today need to have a personal relationship with the one, true God through Jesus the Messiah.

Topic C: Standing Stones

As Christians, our ability to face the future is directly related to our awareness of how God has already worked in our lives. God's work in the past, whether the distant past or our own past, is the foundation on which our beliefs and commitment are built. Thus it is appropriate for God's people to establish "standing stones" as memorials to what God has done. Just as people in the cult of Asclepius inscribed their names and the ailment from which they were healed on standing stones to honor their false god, John described a "white stone with a new name written on it" (Revelation 2:17).

1. For each of the following passages, summarize the story or event mentioned and note the work of God that the standing stone commemorates or represents:

Scripture	Significance of the "Standing Stone"
Genesis 28:10–18	
Joshua 4:1–9	
Joshua 24:19–27	
Revelation 2:12–17	

2. To what does Peter compare believers in 1 Peter 2:4–5?

3. What kind of lives are believers called to live—and why?
   How does this relate to the purpose of "standing stones"?

Topic D: Living in the Place Where Satan Lives

Satan's foremost purpose is to pull people away from God. He accomplishes this by making the pursuit of sin not only acceptable but also appealing, and by robbing God of the credit He alone deserves. Satan can be described as living or having his throne wherever such activities take place.

1. Note the pursuit of evil described elsewhere in Scripture that was also practiced in Pergamum.

   a. 2 Peter 2:9–14, 18–19

   b. 1 Corinthians 10:19–21

   c. 1 Corinthians 6:9

   d. 1 John 3:8

   e. Leviticus 17:10–12; Acts 15:19–20, 29

2. What is the responsibility of believers who live among evil
    people? (See 1 Peter 3:15–17.)

DATA FILE

Five Candidates for "Satan's Throne"

There are many opin-
ions as to exactly
what John referred to
when he wrote these
phrases in Revelation
2:13: "where Satan has
his throne" and "where
Satan lives." No one
knows whether he had
in mind a specific tem-

Altar of Zeus

ple or pagan practice, or whether the sum of the evil activities in Pergamum
made the city the home of Satan. In a sense, all of the following pagan centers could be identified as strongholds of Satan.

The Great Altar of Zeus

Around 250 B.C., the people of Pergamum won a great victory against
the Galatians. In memory of that event, they built a great altar to Zeus, who
was considered to be king of the gods, the life-giver, the lord of all, the creator of all—titles that belong to God alone. Located on the west side of
the Acropolis more than one thousand feet above the valley, the altar of
Zeus smoked day and night with sacrifices. It could be seen from a great
distance and was shaped like an ancient throne. Built on a podium 105 feet
by 110 feet, the forty-foot-high altar was the largest in the world. It had
three tiers with steps on one side, and each tier had a carved marble frieze
featuring scenes of Zeus mythology, which was extremely immoral. Today,
the entire altar is in the Pergamum Museum in Berlin.

(continued on page 72)

(continued from page 71)

Dionysus Temple and Cult Center

Dionysus Temple

Originally built in the third century before Christ, this small, beautiful temple was remodeled by the Romans. It was approached by a twenty-five-step stairway at the end of a 770-foot terrace. Here, people worshiped Dionysus, the fertility god of the vine who was also known as the god of ecstasy, particularly because of the wine he supposedly provided and the orgies related to his worship. During festivals that celebrated him, worshipers consumed wine in great abundance and gorged on raw meat from Dionysus's sacred animal—the bull—all in an effort to be mystically joined to him.

The cult center is believed to have been located on the south side of the Acropolis, near wine shops and a bath house. This center is eighty feet long and thirty-two feet wide. A niche for the idol of Dionysus was positioned to the right of a marble altar. Murals depicting the Dionysus practices were found in frescoes on the low walls around the room. The wine shop next door had several large, baked-clay jars buried in the floor that probably contained wine used in various cultic practices or sold to the public.

Dionysus was considered to be the source of fertility for the grapevines, and one of his symbols was the phallus. He was also viewed as the source of life, so ceremonies dedicated to him included a variety of sexually immoral practices. The cult attracted the common people because it promised eternal life to worshipers and catered to human lusts aroused by the pagan cults. Drunkenness and sexual immorality was so extreme during celebrations in Dionysus's honor that his worship was banned for a time in Rome because it was too perverted! Again, Satan created a counterfeit to take credit for things of God: eternal life, happiness, purpose, and fertility.

Demeter: The Goddess of Groceries

Believed to be the goddess of grain who provided food, Demeter was popular among common people because acquiring enough food was a dominant concern for them. This secretive cult worshiped in a temple (twenty-two by forty feet) and eight-hundred-seat theater complex on the south side of the acropolis of Pergamum. It was also known for its death-resurrection theme that focused on Demeter's daughter who was allowed to spend half the year in Hades and the other half on earth. Thus adherents believed that Demeter offered them the possibility of resurrection.

Although little is known about the rituals of this religion, there was an initiation ceremony involving the blood of a bull. The initiate would stand or lie at the bottom of a pit while a bull was slaughtered above on a grid. The blood would wash over the new convert, providing redemptive cleansing—a clever imitation of salvation through Jesus' shed blood on the cross.

The Cult of Asclepius

The Pool in Asclepion

Asclepius, the god who healed with moving water, was said to be the son of the god Apollo and a woman named Coronis. His symbol was the snake and he was known as the god of life because the snake seemingly resurrects itself (sheds its skin and is born anew, disappears to hibernate and reappears each year). Live snakes were kept in a sacred chest in each of his temples.

Asclepius was also known as "Asclepius Savior." Hospitals or treatment centers were frequently located in conjunction with his temples, and people flocked to Pergamum from all over the world to seek healing at the large Asclepion there. The healing process was a mixture of religious ceremony and health practices—especially diet, water, herbs, and exercise.

When patients entered the Asclepion (hospital) in Pergamum after traveling the kilometer-long "sacred way," they were greeted at the gate

(continued on page 74)

(continued from page 73)

by temple priests who would interview them to determine their accept-ability for healing. Old people and pregnant women nearing the time of delivery were excluded (no deaths or births were allowed within the sanctuary), as were those who were considered impure. This is an inter-esting parallel to modern-day cultures that seek to terminate the lives of senior citizens and the unborn.

Each patient who was admitted made an offering (probably incense) to show his or her devotion to Asclepius and began receiving free, super-vised treatment. As part of the healing process, "sacred water" from a spring and a well was used for bathing and drinking. Treatments included mud baths, special diet, exercise, stress relief, and exposure to the sun. (Perhaps some of the patients' sleep was drug induced.)

Any healing that took place—whether as the result of psychological suggestion, demonic powers, and/or the medical knowledge of the day—was credited to Asclepius. Healed people would bow to the statue of Asclepius and the sacred snake to offer thanks, make an offering—apparently a pig—and have their names and the ailments Asclepius had cured inscribed on a marble pillar (usually white). Finally, each healed person would leave a gift with the priests to thank the god and would witness to many other people about Asclepius's great ability to heal. Thus many people heard or saw the praise and honor given to Asclepius, which in turn increased the cult's popularity.

Emperor Worship

The center of Roman administration of the province of Asia, Perga-mum was also the source and center of emperor worship in the Roman Empire. Julius Caesar was honored with a statue as early as 63 B.C. Emperor Augustus was worshiped in the precinct of Athena, and a bronze statue of the emperor (now in the Vatican Museum) was placed there in 31 B.C., making Pergamum the first city in the empire to have an emperor cult.

On Caesar Augustus's birthday, the people of Pergamum worshiped him with processions, sacrifices, and a choir singing hymns in his honor. Once a year, everyone in the province was commanded to put incense on the altar of "divine" Caesar and declare, "Caesar is lord." This soon led to significant persecution of Christians, who would not make such a declaration because "Jesus is Lord." They refused to give the emperor honor due to God alone. Possibly the martyr Antipas mentioned in Revelation 2:13 was killed for refusing to worship the emperor. He is the only person besides Jesus who is called a "faithful" or "true" witness in the Bible.

Topic E: But It's Just Food!

1. What was the complaint God had against the Christians in Pergamum? (See Revelation 2:14–16.)

2. Why was the eating of food sacrificed to idols of such significance?

   a. In the Old Testament? (See Numbers 25:1–3.)

   b. In the New Testament? (See 1 Corinthians 8:4–13; 10:18–21.)

3. What was so offensive about eating raw meat, meat with blood in it?

   a. In the Old Testament? (See Leviticus 17:10–14.)

   b. In the New Testament? (See Acts 15:19–20, 29.)

4. Identify and discuss our cultural equivalents to eating food sacrificed to idols and eating meat with blood in it—activities that are so strongly associated with a pagan worldview that they must be avoided.

DID YOU KNOW?

In Revelation 2:15, the apostle John condemns those who follow the teachings of Balaam and the Nicolaitans. Balaam is known for his role in encouraging the Israelites to participate in the feasts and sexual immorality of the Canaanite idols, which led them away from God. Scholars disagree about who the Nicolaitans were. According to church tradition, they comprised a group of people who believed that since they were redeemed by Jesus and, therefore, free in Him, they could participate in immoral ceremonies since idols were not gods anyway. Interestingly, both words mean the same thing, "prince of the people." Biblical writers strongly condemned participation in such behavior (1 Corinthians 10:20–22) for many reasons, including the fact that Christians were not to eat meat or drink wine that had been used in sacrifices to pagan gods.

ғɑiтh Lesson

Time for Reflection

Read the following Scripture passage and take the next few minutes to consider how you can do a better job of standing for God in an evil world.

> The acts of the sinful nature are obvious: sexual immorality, impurity and debauchery; idolatry and witchcraft; hatred, discord, jealousy, fits of rage, selfish ambition, dissensions, factions and envy; drunkenness, orgies, and the like. I warn you, as I did before, that those who live like this will not inherit the kingdom of God.
>
> But the fruit of the Spirit is love, joy, peace, patience, kindness, goodness, faithfulness, gentleness and self-control. Against such things there is no law. Those who belong to Christ Jesus have crucified the sinful nature with its passions and desires. Since we live by the Spirit, let us keep in step with the Spirit.
>
> GALATIANS 5:19–25

It's easy to make excuses for sinful behavior that is accepted as "normal" in society. In what ways do you make excuses to indulge in your sinful nature rather than to keep in step with the Spirit?

Consider for a moment the difference in testimony between a Christian who gives into temptations versus one who lives by the Spirit. What kind of an impact would each one have on a watching world?

In what specific areas do you need to reaffirm your submission to Christ's lordship and live more in accordance with His Spirit?

Action Points

Take a moment to jot down an action step (or steps) that you will commit to this week as a result of what you have learned.

1. *The host of pagan gods worshiped in Pergamum encouraged people to seek what they needed for life somewhere other*

than from God. Perhaps that's why John wrote that Satan "lived" in that city, which was noted for its many shrines and temples.

People were drawn to the wine drinking and sexual license as well as the promise of physical healing, provision of food, forgiveness of sins, and immortality. Clearly Satan wanted people to believe that meaning and significance—even eternal life—could be found through themselves, false gods, or the world around them. Satan still offers this temptation to people today.

In what way(s)—even the most subtle—are you tempted to try to find "life" through ways other than God?

Identify the "gods" of this world that appeal most to you. What will you do to strengthen your spiritual "armor" against those specific temptations?

2. *Having been carefully prepared ahead of time by Jesus, John and the other early missionaries knew the truth about Satan's counterfeit blessings.* They knew that God and God alone is the source of all true blessings. John had witnessed Jesus' life and miracles firsthand and was prepared to refute the claims of false religions.

Evaluate your personal preparedness to refute Satan's false claims:

Which of your personal experiences testify to God being the source of all truth and all blessings?

Which false teachings are you equipped to refute by using the Word of God?

3. *Using the imagery of the white stones inscribed by people who supposedly had been healed by Asclepius, John challenged believers in Pergamum to stand courageously as witnesses for God, telling what He had done in their lives and giving Him the credit He was due.*

Believers today have the important responsibility of expressing God's truth to a spiritually hungry world. We need to let people know what God has done for us and praise God for all that He has done—the "ordinary" as well as the extraordinary.

What specifically can you say that God has done for you?

In what ways have you given Him credit and praise for what He has done?

In what ways have you given the credit to someone or something other than God?

What specific action might you take to become a standing stone for another person—to communicate to him or her what God has done?

The Mark of the Beast

Questions to Think About

1. What happens when you share your Christian beliefs with non-Christians who are offended by your beliefs? How do you feel and respond when they challenge your faith?

2. What kinds of situations lead you to become "weary" in your Christian walk? What strengthens or encourages you during those "weary" times?

3. Imagine that you and a few new believers are the only Christians in your city, that its people don't want you to speak publicly about your faith, and that unless you proclaim allegiance to their view of the world, you will lose your job, you won't be able to buy food, your water and electricity will be shut off, and you might even be killed. What would you do? How would you live?

video notes

Ephesus, Crown Jewel of Asia

Artemis of the Ephesians

Paul Begins to Teach

The Implications of God's Truth

Who Is Lord and God?

A Legacy of Christian Love

video Highlights

1. Locate Ephesus on the map of Asia Minor below. Why would Ephesus have been an important city even if it hadn't been the world center for the worship of Artemis and the Roman Emperor Domitian?

2. What do you imagine it would have been like to live as a Christian in Ephesus?

Asia Minor

3. Why do you think God was able to use Paul and the other Christians in Ephesus in such significant ways?

4. What did it mean for the Ephesian Christians to choose who—God or the Roman emperor—was Lord in their lives? What does this suggest to Christians today who desire Christ to be Lord?

small Group Bible Discovery

Topic A: Paul's Ministry in Ephesus

As we better understand Paul's ministry in Ephesus, we learn what other early believers there faced and how God used them to spread His message to the world. We also see that the truth of the gospel message always undermines the beliefs of paganism, which often prompts a negative reaction from unbelievers.

1. Read Acts 19:8–12.

    a. Where and for how long did Paul teach in Ephesus?

b. What did Paul proclaim in Ephesus, and how did he demonstrate God's power over Satan?

2. For which two things was Ephesus famous, and how did the implications of the gospel affect these practices?

a. Acts 19:18–20

b. Acts 19:23–27

3. What kind of temple for the true God did exist in Ephesus? (See Ephesians 2:19–22.)

PROFILE OF A MAN-MADE GODDESS: ARTEMIS

Who was Artemis?	The supposed goddess of fertility.
Who worshiped her?	She was probably the most-worshiped deity in Asia and perhaps the world during Paul's time.
What was worship like?	Hundreds of eunuch priests, virgin priestesses, and religious prostitutes served her. Worship rituals were quite erotic.
By what other names was Artemis known?	"Queen of Heaven," "Savior," and "Mother Goddess."
What role did Ephesus have in Artemis worship?	Ephesus was considered *neokorus* for Artemis, which meant the city was the center for Artemis worship and was responsible for maintaining the cult's purity of worship.
How did Ephesus benefit financially from the worship of Artemis?	The cult brought great wealth to the citizens of Ephesus because the temple of Artemis became the world's largest bank during that time.
What were Artemis festivals like?	Devotees came from all over the world to worship and celebrate during her festivals. Huge processions honored her statues. Celebrations were held with music, dancing, singing, dramatic presentations, and chanting of allegiance.
What were Artemis statues like?	They portrayed Artemis as having many breasts—a symbol of her fertility. The main statue in her temple may have been a black meteorite because she was said to have fallen from the sky.
What was the Artemis temple like?	The temple was one of the seven wonders of the ancient world.
How else do we know that Artemis was important to Ephesus?	Two statues of her have been found in the Prytaneion—the "city hall" of Ephesus— indicating that she was considered to be the basis for life in the city.
What attracted people to Artemis?	The promise of fertility, long life, sexual fullfillment, and protection during pregnancy and childbirth; the seductive sexuality of her worship.

DATA FILE

The Theater at Ephesus

In the world of the early believers, the theater was a significant institution for communicating the Hellenistic view of the world. Every major city in the Roman world had a theater, and the theater in Ephesus was spectacular. The Greek king Lysimachus originally built the theater in Ephesus during the third century B.C. Emperor Claudius (A.D. 41–54) enlarged it, and Emperor Nero (A.D. 54–68) continued renovations.

The ruins remaining demonstrate how impressive the theater in Ephesus once was. It had three tiers of seats and could hold an estimated twenty-five thousand people. The stage was 130 feet wide and 80 feet deep. Imagine how the theater must have roared when thousands of devotees of the goddess Artemis became angry at Paul and shouted praises to their goddess for two hours!

Although the stage building is mostly gone, it's interesting to note that the audience in Ephesus preferred no backdrop to the stage. They wanted to see life in the city beyond. The drama that took place on the

(continued on page 88)

The Theater at Ephesus

(continued from page 87)

stage portrayed the way the Ephesians viewed themselves; it was a reflection of their lives. In another sense, the drama portrayed the goal for which the culture was striving—who the people wanted to be. So, the people preferred to look beyond the stage to what was happening in their community.

Theaters such as the one in Ephesus were used for both entertainment and religious festivals. Regular plays—dramas (often portraying the myths of the gods), comedies, satires—typically began with sacrifices to Dionysus (the god of theater) and other deities in order to dedicate the presentation to the gods.

During a festival honoring a particular god or goddess, a procession would begin at the god's temple and parade through Ephesus. Led by priests, priestesses, and cult members, the celebrants and pilgrims would carry the symbols and statues of their deity. Passersby would honor the god with gifts or by placing incense on altars placed along the route. The procession typically ended at the theater, where the statues were placed on pedestals and worshiped. People then gave speeches, sacrificed animals, and offered the meat on altars in the stage area. Faithful devotees would then eat the roasted or boiled meat, symbolizing their communion with the deity.

Thus, it became difficult, if not impossible, for Christians in Ephesus to frequent the theater. They would not participate in the sacrifices before dramatic presentations, were offended by stories of gods that the human imagination had created, and refused to eat meat sacrificed to gods that represented demonic powers. No doubt the citizens of Ephesus hated the Christians—not so much for their beliefs but for their refusal to compromise and honor the deities that other people worshiped. As emperor worship became more prevalent, Christians risked their lives to avoid such celebrations.

Topic B: Emperor Worship in Ephesus

Long before the Romans or Paul came to Ephesus, the people of Asia Minor had considered their rulers to be divine. Croesus, king of Sardis (around 550 B.C.), was honored as a divine king. Alexander the Great declared that he was a descendant of Heracles and Zeus and was therefore divine. Inhabitants of the cities he conquered were delighted to consider him a god and honored him with statues, festivals, and regular sacrifices. So the people of Asia Minor did not balk when the Roman Emperors, starting with Caesar Augustus, began making claims to be divine.

As the early Christians began spreading the gospel message throughout Asia Minor, emperor worship was growing rapidly. In Ephesus, Domitian, who was obsessed with his claim to deity, built a huge temple dedicated to himself and enforced his worship under the threat of death. The Ephesians were required to declare Caesar as lord and to sprinkle incense on an altar to indicate their allegiance to him. They were also expected to sacrifice to the emperor and eat sacrificed meat. Severe penalties existed for anyone who refused to publicly acknowledge that Caesar was lord. So Ephesus became a dangerous place for Christians, who would declare no one other than Jesus the Messiah to be Lord.

1. What event concluded Jesus' final forty days on earth after His resurrection? What did this event reveal about Jesus in light of the growing emperor-worship cult? (See Acts 1:1–11.)

2. In 1 Timothy 1:3, Paul writes that he wants Timothy to stay
    in Ephesus in order to stand against certain men who
    taught false doctrine. Based on the points Paul emphasized
    in 1 Timothy 6:11–16, what might have been the nature
    of his concern?

3. In what ways does the fact that Roman emperors
    demanded to be worshiped as "lord" add to the meaning of
    the following verses?

    a. Romans 10:9

    b. Philippians 2:5–11

DID YOU KNOW?

A Roman emperor was declared to be divine when a witness came forward claiming to have seen the emperor ascend to heaven or claiming to have seen the emperor's father ascend to heaven (making the current emperor the "Son of God"). This process was called *apotheosis*.

4. Why was King Herod struck down by God, and what might this event have taught the believers in Ephesus who had to confront emperor worship? (See Acts 12:21–24.)

5. What was Paul's prayer for the Ephesian believers, who faced persecution from people who worshiped the Roman emperor and other false gods? (See Ephesians 3:14–21.)

FACTS TO CONSIDER

The Demands of Emperor Worship

Every person in Ephesus and other cities that worshiped the emperor was expected to:

- Participate in festivals honoring the emperor(s). This included offering incense on altars carried by priests to declare that Caesar was Lord, making sacrifices to the emperor, and eating sacrificed meat.
- Offer incense to Caesar before entering the city.
- To obey Caesar without question.
- To acknowledge the authority of the emperor when conducting business or shopping in the market. They were to stop at his altars to acknowledge his "lordship," had to acknowledge the emperor as the provider of life before drawing water from public fountains, etc.

DATA FILE

The Temple of Domitian

Built on the slope of the hill south of Ephesus and extending into the center of the city, this prominent temple could be seen from nearly everywhere in Ephesus, including the land and harbor entrances. The Ephesians, who built it to honor their emperor in order to gain the greatest benefits from him, pressured other Ephesians and the province of Asia Minor to declare the emperor "Lord and God."

Huge columns more than thirty-five feet high supported the two-hundred-by-three-hundred-foot podium on which the temple of Domitian rested. One unusual feature is that these columns had carvings that represented various deities. Apparently the Ephesians designed the podium this way in order to declare that the emperor was supported by all the world's gods and that he was the culmination of all deity—the final lord of heaven and earth, the god of gods.

Although not large, the forty-by-sixty-foot temple had four columns in the front and a row of columns around the outside (eight in front and back, thirteen on the sides). A large, marble altar stood on a raised platform and had a U-shaped colonnade around it with the open end facing the temple. On altars such as this one, the people were required to sprinkle incense to declare that Caesar was lord.

Temple of Domitian

A statue of what is believed to be Domitian stood near the temple and altar. Based on the huge arm and head that have been excavated, researchers believe the statue was twenty-seven feet tall. After Domitian died, he was discredited by the Roman senate, and the temple was rededicated to his beloved father, Vespasian, who was emperor from A.D. 69–79. Today, the ruins reveal the emperors' great earthly glory and also declare the futility of denying the lordship of the God of the Bible.

Head and Arm from Domitian Statue

Topic C: Living as Witnesses in an Evil Culture

With a population of nearly 250,000 and a reputation for being the richest city in the world, Ephesus was a trend-setting place—not unlike New York City or Los Angeles today. Its seaport, which provided a key link in the Roman world between the east (Persia, Syria, Judea, Egypt) and the west (Greece, Rome), made it a center of political and commercial power. Ephesus was a stronghold of Satanic power as well. People came from all over the world to worship the goddess Artemis, many people were demon possessed, people practiced magic and sorcery, and emperor worship was celebrated. Despite these seeming obstacles, the gospel message found fertile ground in this powerful, pagan city.

1. What did God do to demonstrate His power over evil in Ephesus? (See Acts 19:11–12.)

2. People in Ephesus were fascinated by the power Paul wielded as he accomplished God's work. Read Acts 19:13–20 to discover the impact God's power had on the people of Ephesus.

   a. Which event terrified the Jews and Greeks who lived in Ephesus? Why do you think this terrified them?

   b. What impact did this incident have on Ephesian believers who had been dabbling in sorcery?

3. In contrast to their pagan neighbors, how were the Ephesian believers to live? (See Ephesians 5:8–12, 15–20.)

4. At the end of his letter to the Ephesian believers, Paul offers advice on how they could continue to live for God in the face of great evil. Read Ephesians 6:10–18 and answer the following questions.

a. Who did Paul say the believers were really fighting as they shared the gospel message? (See verses 10–12.)

b. How did Paul say the Ephesian believers could stand their ground? (See verse 13.)

DATA FILE

The Sign of the Fish—*ixthus*

Early Christian believers often used the "fish" symbol. This may be because Jesus called His disciples to be "fishers of men" (Matthew 4:19). Or, perhaps the Greek word for fish, *ixthus*, was an acrostic for Jesus Christ, Son of God, Savior:

i—first letter in the Greek word for "Jesus"
x—first letter in the Greek word for "Christ"
th—first letter in the Greek word for "God"
u—first letter in the Greek word for "son"
s—first letter in the Greek word for "savior"

WORTH OBSERVING . . .

Called to Pursue Our "First Love"

According to Matthew 22:37–38, believers in Jesus the Messiah are to love the Lord their God with all their heart, soul, and mind (strength). Yet, according to Romans 13:8–10, 1 John 2:9–11, 1 John 3:10–11, and other biblical passages, love for other people is the preeminent sign that a person loves God. Thus, as believers, we are called to love other people. This is the first love that occurs when one is in relationship with God.

Love, in fact, distinguishes the community of God's people from people who do not love God. When Paul wrote to the Ephesian believers (probably around A.D. 54), he mentioned their love for one another (Ephesians 1:15–16) and encouraged loving unity in the body of Christ (Ephesians 4:15–16). Their love for one another is perhaps one reason the church in Ephesus had such an impact in such an evil place. But later, God warned the Ephesians that they had forsaken their "first love" (Revelation 2:1–7). This implies that they may have become divided over theological issues.

Unfortunately, many Christians today focus more on their disagreements than they do on simply loving one another. Could that be one reason why the church as a whole is so fractured today, why our witness for Jesus has been greatly weakened, and why the Christian community as a whole is not as effective today as it was in Ephesus?

Topic D: *Chutzpah*

The apostles were so persistent in teaching and living out Jesus' message because they were totally convinced that Jesus was the Messiah and He had prepared them well to carry His message to the world. But there is another reason they were so effective, and that has to do with their understanding of their faith.

In the Jewish culture of that time, the word *faith* had many meanings. One meaning was "bold persistence, unyielding intensity that will not give up." That's what the Hebrew word *chutzpah* meant. Thus, the early believers were bold, determined, persistent, and unwilling to be stopped in their service to God. (It did not mean they were to be overly pushy, negatively aggressive, or disrespectful toward anyone, which is a connotation the word has in our culture.) Let's consider how the Jewish understanding of faith helped spread the gospel to the world.

1. According to the following verses, what was the early Christians' (including those in Ephesus) fundamental source of boldness?

Scripture	Source of *Chutzpah*
2 Timothy 1:6–7	
Acts 1:8	
Acts 4:29–31	

2. According to Luke 11:5–8, why did the man finally receive the bread he needed? What did Jesus teach about *chutzpah* through this parable?

3. How did Abraham demonstrate *chutzpah* in Genesis 18:16–33?

4. In Ephesus, a key center of idol worship, how did Paul demonstrate *chutzpah*? (See Acts 19:8–10; Ephesians 6:19–20.)

DID YOU KNOW?

People *Will* Respond to God's Truth

The Word of God is true, and we can confidently share the gospel message with anyone. But God's truth is also powerful and it *will* make an impact—at times it will turn people's hearts toward God and at other times it will bring us into conflict with people who deny God's truth.

Situation	What Happened
Peter shared God's truth with the crowd at Pentecost (Acts 2:14–41).	About three thousand people received God's truth and became Christians.
Peter and John healed a beggar and shared the gospel message with people near the temple in Jerusalem (Acts 3–4:4; 4:18–21).	The religious leaders seized Peter and John and threw them into prison; about five thousand men who heard God's truth became Christians. The leaders then commanded Peter and John to stop preaching; they refused and were let go.
Philip preached God's truth to the followers of Simon the Sorcerer (Acts 8:9–13).	Simon and many of his followers became believers and were baptized.
Paul and Barnabas preached in Pisidian Antioch to almost the entire city (Acts 13:42–52).	Jealous Jews attacked what Paul was saying, Paul and Silas boldly answered them, and God's Word spread throughout the entire region. Paul and Barnabas were then expelled from the region.

Paul and Silas boldly preached in the Jewish temple in Iconium for quite a long time (Acts 14:1–7).	Many Jews and Gentiles became believers, but unbelieving Jews stirred up the people. Finally, upon learning that they were to be killed, Paul and Silas left the city and preached in other places.
After casting an evil spirit out of a girl, Paul and Silas were thrown into prison, where they prayed and sang hymns to God. After God delivered them from prison, they preached to the jailer and his household (Acts 16:16–34).	The jailer and all his family became believers and were baptized.
Paul spoke to the Corinthians in the house of Titius Justus and kept on teaching the Word of God for a year and a half (Acts 18:7 17).	The synagogue ruler in Corinth, his entire household, and many Corinthians became believers. The Jews took Paul to court, complaining that he was causing people to worship God in ways contrary to the law. The case was thrown out of court.

THE TRUTH OF THE MATTER:

The Importance of Acknowledging Jesus as Lord

As the early church grew, believers had two choices: (1) to go along with the pagan world in order to not create offense and endanger themselves and their families; or (2) to stand firm and declare that Jesus was Lord and risk suffering—even death. The witness of the believers was a declaration of war on the Roman state and its Satanic foundation. Here, two worldviews competed for domination of the world, and there could be no compromise.

Today, believers face a similar choice. Will they totally submit to the Lordship of Jesus regardless of the cost? Will they serve Him everywhere and in everything, whether the cost is economic, social, or even life itself? Jesus is Lord. The battle is not between believers and pagan authorities. Rather, it is between Jesus and Satan, and the outcome of that battle has already been determined. (See Revelation 20.)

faith Lesson

Time for Reflection

Read the following passage of Scripture and take the next few minutes to consider the ways in which you can live out and proclaim the gospel message to your world.

> Finally, be strong in the Lord and in his mighty power. Put on the full armor of God so that you can take your stand against the devil's schemes. . . . Pray also for me, that whenever I open my mouth, words may be given me so that I will fearlessly make known the mystery of the gospel, for which I am an ambassador in chains. Pray that I may declare it fearlessly, as I should.
>
> Ephesians 6:10–11, 19–20

Christians today generally think of the apostle Paul as being fearless—the boldest of the bold—in proclaiming the message of Jesus the Messiah. Yet as he closes his letter to the Ephesians, he asks them to pray that he will be fearless in proclaiming the gospel. What does that tell you about Paul and what it takes to truly live for Jesus in an evil world?

As you consider your life and the way in which God has called you to live out and proclaim His truth, for what do you need the prayers of others?

Who can you ask to pray for you in this way?

For whom can you pray for in this way?

Consider the Christians throughout the world who are being persecuted for their faith. What can you do to educate yourself concerning the nature of that persecution so that you can pray for their needs as they seek to "stand against the devil's schemes"?

Action Points

Take a moment to jot down an action step (or steps) that you will commit to this week as a result of what you have learned.

1. In ancient Ephesus, the spiritual battle lines were clearly drawn. Satan offered false gods such as Artemis and the worship of Roman emperors such as Domitian to challenge the lordship of Jesus the Messiah. *In the face of intense persecution, the Ephesian Christians had to choose whom they would serve—and they chose Jesus. They refused to acknowledge the lordship of anyone but God.*

    What powers or idols challenge the lordship of Christ in your life?

    If Christ is anything less than Lord of your life, what steps will you take to restore Him to His rightful place?

2. *With a passionate, fearless faith in God, Paul and other Christians in Ephesus were unashamed to publicly live out and tirelessly proclaim the truth of God.* Their focus was not to undermine the beliefs of others, but to lovingly and boldly reveal what had been revealed to them. The implications of that truth spoke to people's hearts and minds with such power and conviction that the Bible tells us "all . . . who lived in the province of Asia" heard the gospel message.

    What one thing have you learned from the early believers' bold and persistent determination to speak out for Jesus that will help you in your efforts to share Jesus with the world around you?

In what ways do the words *boldness, courage, passion, fearlessness, hard work, faith,* and *perseverance* characterize your public Christian life? What must you do so that they will be more descriptive of your life?

3. *The Ephesian believers were known for their love for one another. That love and support helped give them the strength to live consistently, publicly, courageously, and faithfully for Jesus in a city that was openly hostile toward them.*

In what way(s) might you become more committed to a community of believers who need your love and support and will love and encourage you so that together you can proclaim the kingdom of God?

Hot or cold

questions to think about

1. Which historical, geographic, or common cultural experiences could you use to help a nonbeliever in your community understand some aspect of the gospel message, or to encourage another believer in his or her walk with God?

2. Think about people who have had the greatest influence on your life for Jesus. What was it about them that touched you deeply?

3. If you were to go out and make a difference, change the world, and impact your culture for Jesus, how would you go about doing it?

4. If Jesus were to show up at your doorstep tomorrow morning, in what way(s) do you think He'd invite you to reach out to people in your community?

video notes

Hierapolis

The Domitian Gate

The Theater

The Apollo Temple and Plutonium

The Baths

Colosse and Its Water

Laodicea and Its Water

Changing the World by Being Hot *and* Cold

video Highlights

1. Locate the cities of Laodicea, Hierapolis, and Colosse on the map of Asia Minor and the Lycus River Valley on page 106 of your participant's guide. Note that Hierapolis is six miles and Colosse is eleven miles away from Laodicea. What surprised you about these cities?

2. When you first heard John's words to the Laodicean church, what did you think the terms "hot" and "cold" meant?

3. In what ways does the possibility that a Christian should be both "hot" *and* "cold" change your perspective?

4. If you had been a Christian living in Hierapolis, what choices might you have had to make on a daily basis in order to live out and proclaim the gospel message?

5. What do you think enabled disciples such as Philip to be successful in proclaiming the gospel and changing the world of Asia Minor?

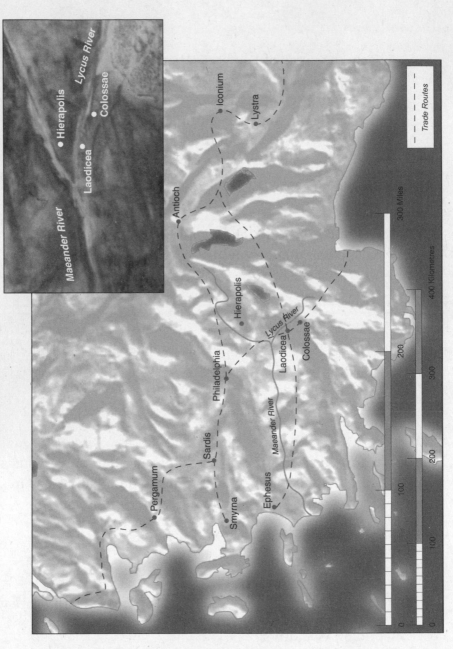

Lycus River Valley

Lycus River
Hierapolis
Colossae
Laodicea
Maeander River

Iconium
Lystra
Antioch
Hierapolis
Lycus River
Laodicea
Colossae
Philadelphia
Maeander River
Sardis
Smyrna
Ephesus
Pergamum

Trade Routes

300 Miles
400 Kilometres
200
300
100
200
100
0
0

DATA FILE

If This Theater Could Talk

The first-century theater of Hierapolis, one of the best-preserved theaters in Asia, clearly demonstrates the city's sophistication at the time Epaphras founded a church there. The carvings below the stage, which was twelve feet high, are in remarkable condition. They depict the mythology of Apollo and Artemis and clearly show the connection between the theater and the worship of pagan gods. This particular theater had seating for seventeen thousand spectators, and in the center of the seating area was a "royal box" from which dignitaries watched events.

Theater at Hierapolis

The Greeks and Romans considered the theater to be more than entertainment. It displayed the ideals of the Hellenistic culture, communicating to people that "This is who we are, and this is who we should become." That's why Greek theaters such as this one were built so that the audience could see the actors on the stage against the backdrop of their communities.

For Christians of that day, the theater created a dilemma. There was nothing inherently sinful about drama, nor were all the presentations there an insult to godly values. But as an institution, the theater presented a seductive argument for the pagan lifestyle. The plays were dedicated to the gods before they began and were used to shape the values and beliefs of those who aspired to be all that a Greek or Roman should be.

Timeline of Events in and around Asia Minor

2000–1000 B.C.	Hittite Empire
920–586 B.C.	Divided kingdom of Israel
586 B.C.	Babylonian captivity
500 B.C.	Jews' return from captivity
325 B.C.	Alexander the Great's conquest
261 B.C.	Laodicea founded
220 B.C.	Antiochus settles Jews from Babylon in Asia
133 B.C.	Roman Empire begins; lasts until A.D. 300
27 B.C.–A.D. 14	Augustus
A.D. 37–41	Caligula (enforced emperor worship)
@ A.D. 48–49	Paul's second missionary journey (Ephesus)
@ A.D. 60	Paul is martyred
A.D. 60	Earthquake damages Laodicea, Hierapolis, and Colosse
@ A.D. 68–78	John is in Asia
A.D. 81–96	Domitian/emperor worship in Ephesus
A.D. 90–100	The book of Revelation written between these dates
A.D. 98–117	Trajan
@ A.D. 110	John's death
@ A.D. 325	Christianity becomes state religion
A.D. 363	A significant church council held in Laodicea

small Group Bible Discovery

Topic A: Faithful *Talmidim*

God provides opportunities for His followers to witness for Him. To be a *talmid* means to be prepared and committed to respond to those opportunities and to be faithful in trusting God to provide the right words and actions. Based on church history, it appears that Philip—one of Jesus' disciples—was God's messenger in Hierapolis. We also know from the Bible that Epaphras, another determined follower of Jesus, probably founded the churches of Laodicea, Hierapolis, and Colosse.

1. What do the following verses reveal about Philip's commitment to being a *talmid* of Jesus?

Scripture	Philip, *talmid* of Jesus the Rabbi
Mark 3:13–19	
John 1:43–49	
John 12:20–22	

2. Read John 6:1–14 and 14:6–14. In what ways would these two situations have prepared Philip for his later ministry?

3. What do the following passages reveal about Epaphras and his work on behalf of the gospel?

Scripture	Epaphras, faithful messenger of the gospel
Colossians 1:1–8	
Philemon 23	
Colossians 4:12–13	

THE TRUTH OF THE MATTER

Confronting the Hellenism of Today

"Man," said the Greek philosopher Protagoras (481–411 B.C.), "is the measure of all things of what is and what is not." This philosophy provided the foundation for Hellenism, which was devoted to the supremacy of human beings and human accomplishment. The cultural tradition of the Greeks, Hellenism was the prevalent worldview before and during the growth of early Christianity.

Hellenism was based on the belief that human beings are the ultimate source of truth and authority in the universe. Since the human being was considered the "measure of all," human wisdom was deemed to be the greatest wisdom. What could not be understood or explained was viewed as false. Human accomplishments in athletics, the arts, and architecture became the motivating drive of society. The human body was considered the ultimate in beauty, so nudity in art, in the baths, and in sport was common. The accumulation of material possessions in order to provide oneself with luxury and comfort was a common pursuit. What could be more natural than to get the most out of life? After all, life's greatest goal was to be the best at any pursuit.

The Hellenists tried to build their society on their gods, which were human creations. In effect, they worshiped themselves. Because they had nothing greater than themselves on which to base their worldview and society, their society eventually collapsed. No society can exist for very long when it creates its own view of truth.

Was Hellenism, at its roots, really new? No. The first evidence of it is recorded when Satan asked Eve, "Did God really say . . . ?" (see Genesis 3:1). Eve, and then Adam, faced an earth-shaking choice: who, or what, was the ultimate source of truth in the universe? When Adam and Eve decided to disobey God's command not to eat from the tree (Genesis 2:16–17), they decided for themselves what was right and best for them and didn't depend on God. They crowned themselves as the ultimate authority in the universe.

In contrast, the worldview of Christianity is based on God as the ultimate truth and authority. His revelation is the source of our vision for society, our knowledge, our morality, and even truth itself. The resulting values are absolute—not merely creations of our imaginations—and form a strong basis for society and the belief in the dignity of each person who is created in God's image. In such a worldview, God is the ultimate authority in the universe. Life is to be lived for Him, not for ourselves. God has created the ultimate in beauty, not humankind. Truth is what God has revealed and allowed people to discover.

The core beliefs of Hellenism haven't disappeared with the advancements of today's culture. Today Hellenism is called Humanism, and it still promotes the idea that the human being is the ultimate authority in the universe. Thus truth is what the human mind can discover, demonstrate, and understand. The glorification of human accomplishment, the drive to be number one, the obsession with comfort and pleasure, the focus on the human body and sexuality, the lack of compassion for other people, and the commitment to the will of the majority as being right are built on a foundation that is as old as the Garden of Eden and was well articulated by ancient Greek philosophers.

Today we commonly hear such phrases as: "Just do it." "If it feels good, who can tell you it's wrong for you?" "I have the right to choose what to

(continued on page 112)

(continued from page 111)

do with my body." Within our public educational system, Hellenistic teaching is prevalent. Truth is defined as that which each person can logically understand and demonstrate (or at least that which the majority of people decides is right).

What does this mean to believers today? We live in the same type of world as the early Christian missionaries did. Our great task, then, is to declare that God alone is supreme and to obey Him. Our great temptation is that we may compromise and live as Hellenists or Humanists—and lose the opportunity to bring God's life-transforming love and truth to a spiritually needy world.

Topic B: Called to Be a Healing Influence

In the world of the early church, hot baths were a key source of health care. People sought healing by bathing or ingesting the hot, mineral-filled water of Hierapolis. John's metaphor of "hot" (Revelation 3:15) was probably drawn from these baths, which could be seen from Laodicea.

1. What did Jesus promise His followers would do? (See John 14:12.)

2. What does James 5:13–16 reveal about the power of Christ's followers to bring about healing?

3. What is the nature and source of the gift of healing, and why is it given? (See 1 Corinthians 12:7–12, 27–28.)

4. Read Matthew 25:31–46 and write down six types of healing in which believers are to be involved.

5. What other kinds of healing do believers provide, according to the following verses?

    a. Colossians 3:12–13

    b. 2 Corinthians 1:3–5

Topic C: Thirsty for God's Living Water

A key point of this session hinges on the imagery of water—the ice-cold water of Colosse, the warm water of Hierapolis, and the foul-tasting, lukewarm water of Laodicea. The imagery of water is used frequently in Scripture as it is in Revelation 3. As you study the following passages, consider the ways in which the world-famous water of Colosse is an image of what followers of Jesus have to offer to others.

1. David's psalms are known for their vivid descriptions of the human longing for God. Note the ways in which David expressed his desire for God in Psalm 42:1–2; 63:1. What do these descriptions tell us about our need for God?

Waterfall of Colosse

2. What incredible, awesome promise does God make to spiritually thirsty people? (See Isaiah 41:17–18.)

3. What was Jesus describing when He answered the Samaritan woman's question at the well? What was her response? (See John 4:10–15, also verses 16–42.)

4. What did Jesus promise to people in Jerusalem? (See John 7:37–39.)

5. According to Isaiah 32:1–2, what are righteous people— those who drink the living water of God—compared to and called to be?

Topic D: Light and Darkness

To people in the ancient world, light and darkness held great meaning, so the Bible makes many references to light and darkness. Perhaps one reason the apostle John used the concept of "light" more than thirty times when writing to the church in Asia Minor is because the god Apollo was considered to be the god of music, prophecy, and light. Let's consider how the concept of light and darkness was used to communicate God's message to the people of Asia Minor.

1. To what was God compared in 2 Samuel 22:29?

2. What imagery did Isaiah use when he predicted the coming of the Messiah? (See Isaiah 9:2.)

3. What did Paul urge the Ephesian Christians to do? (See
    Ephesians 5:8–14.)

4. As the Colossian Christians read Paul's letter, probably
    within sight of the Apollo temple of Hierapolis that
    adjoined the "Gates of Hades," what were they urged to
    do? (See Colossians 1:12–14.)

5. Keeping in mind that Apollo was considered to be the god
    of light, yet was a counterfeit god who kept people in spir-
    itual darkness, read John 8:12. How do you think follow-
    ers of Apollo would have responded to what Jesus said
    about Himself?

6. What do you think it meant to the disciples when Jesus
    told them they were "the light of the world"? How might
    they have responded to followers of Apollo? (See Matthew
    5:14–16.)

DATA FILE

The Temple of Apollo in Hierapolis

Located on the main street between the theater and a sacred pool, this forty-by-sixty-foot temple was dedicated to the supposed god of light, Apollo. The entrance faced west and was approached by a broad flight of stairs.

Beneath the Temple of Apollo is the Plutonium, the cave that people believed led to the underworld. Pluto (or Hades, as the Greeks called him), was viewed as the god of the underworld and supposedly came and went via the opening to the cave, which was next to the temple.

The Plutonium played an important role in the culture of that day. Strabo, a Roman writer, described the fenced plaza in front of the cave opening where ceremonies took place. No doubt the consequences of entering the cave had much to do with its importance. All animals and most people, except the priests of the gods, died instantly if they entered it and breathed its poisonous gases. No one knows how the priests survived—perhaps they held their breath or had an unknown source of fresh air. Even today poisonous gases seep out of the cave, so its entrance is blocked by a fence to protect the unwary.

Apollo Temple

Topic E: The Church in Colosse

Although the city of Colosse was in decline, this city of cold, fresh, rushing water had a vibrant Christian community.

1. Who founded the church in Colosse? (See Acts 19:8–10; Colossians 1:1–7)

2. How well did Paul know the Colossian believers? (See Colossians 1:3–4.)

3. The brief letter of Philemon is addressed to one of the leaders of the church in Colosse. Note what it reveals about the believers there.

   a. What had Paul heard about them and what impact did it have on him? (See Philemon 1–7.)

   b. What did Paul ask the Colossians to do? (See Philemon 6.)

   c. What did Paul specifically ask Philemon to do, and what did he expect would be the outcome? (See Philemon 10–22.)

4. According to Colossians 2:8, 16–21, which challenges was
    the church facing?

DATA FILE

Laodicea

History
The leading city in the valley during the first century, Laodicea was destroyed by an earthquake in A.D. 60. According to Roman writer Tacitus, Rome offered to pay for the city to be rebuilt, but the people declined, saying that they were wealthy enough to restore their own city.

Industry
The city was renowned for three main industries:
- a banking center for the province of Asia Minor, including a gold exchange;
- the textile center where glossy, black wool was woven into garments called *trimata* that were prized in the Roman world;
- the location of a major medical school known worldwide and where an eye salve called Phyrigian powder was made from a local stone.

Encrusted Stone Water Pipes of Laodicea

Geography
Located in the fertile Lycus River Valley, the city had no nearby water source, so tepid, mineral-filled, and nauseating water was piped in from six miles away.

DID YOU KNOW?

What Happened to the Church in Laodicea?

Church history records that the church in Laodicea remained dynamic after most churches in Asia disappeared. One of its bishops was martyred for his faith in A.D. 161, about seventy years after John wrote his warning to the city in the book of Revelation. In A.D. 363, Laodicea was the location chosen for a significant church council. So, it appears that the church in Laodicea learned its lesson and God continued to bless the Christian community there for some time.

faith Lesson

Time for Reflection

Read the following passage of Scripture and take the next few minutes to consider what this passage may have meant to the believers in Laodicea and what it means for Christians today.

> "To the angel of the church in Laodicea write:
> These are the words of the Amen, the faithful and true witness, the ruler of God's creation. I know your deeds, that you are neither cold nor hot. I wish you were either one or the other! So, because you are lukewarm—neither hot nor cold—I am about to spit you out of my mouth. You say, 'I am rich; I have acquired wealth and do not need a thing.' But you do not realize that you are wretched, pitiful, poor, blind and naked. I counsel you to buy from me gold refined in the fire, so you can become rich; and white clothes to wear, so you can cover your shameful nakedness; and salve to put on your eyes, so you can see.
> Those whom I love I rebuke and discipline. So be earnest, and repent.

· Revelation 3:14–19

God's inspired Word speaks to all people. Although a person can understand the Bible without knowing the cultural settings in which particular books were written, one can learn even more by learning the common images and symbols the biblical writers used. The apostle John used a number of metaphors from history, culture, and geography in his Revelation 3 letter to the church in Laodicea. Based on what you've learned in this session, consider what these metaphors meant to the people and what they mean to you today:

Phrase Used	What This Phrase May Have Referred To
You are neither cold	
...nor hot	
Because you are lukewarm	
I am about to spit you out of my mouth	
You say, "I am rich; I have acquired wealth and do not need a thing"	
But you do not realize you are wretched, pitiful, poor, blind and naked	
I counsel you to buy from me gold refined in the fire	
White clothes to wear	
Salve to put on your eyes, so you can see	

If you were to describe a type of water to symbolize your walk with God right now, consider the kind of water you would choose. Would it be stagnant? A fast-flowing mountain stream? A clear, sparkling pool? A warm bath? A thundering waterfall?

Action Points

Take a moment to jot down an action step (or steps) that you will commit to this week as a result of what you have learned.

1. *John, when writing to the church in Laodicea, used images of the Laodiceans' everyday world in order to communicate God's message.* He referred to what the Laodiceans had told the Roman emperor who wanted to help them rebuild their city. He mentioned blindness to a city whose key industry was making and marketing eye salve. And he described their faith in terms of the local water—the most basic necessity of life.

   Which commonly understood images of culture are you able to use in communicating God's message to spiritually needy people?

   In what specific ways might you use your background, training, and/or interests to better communicate the message of Jesus to your world?

2. *God longs for those who follow Him to be wholehearted and passionate in offering His message to a hurting world.* Like the water of Colosse, which was cold, fresh, and invigorating, followers of Christ offer a message that is refreshing to hearts that are weary of sin. Like the warm, healing mineral waters of Hierapolis, followers of Christ offer a message that brings healing to those who are wounded and broken by sin. And like the nauseating, tepid water of Laodicea, followers who do nothing, who are neither hot nor cold, turn God's stomach.

   What's your temperature?

   In which practical ways can you be more like hot water, bringing healing and comfort to hurting people? To whom?

   In which ways can you be more like cold water, sharing encouragement through the empowering, caring love of Jesus the Messiah? To whom?

3. *Using what Jesus had taught them, or what they had learned through other believers, early Christians such as Philip passionately proclaimed the gospel throughout the Roman world. Consequently, God used them to change that world!* Christians today have no less of an opportunity to

live as Jesus' disciples and bring His message to a lost and hurting world.

Do you believe that God can use you to change your world?

Identify some aspect of your faith—your knowledge of God's Word, your walk with God—that you can be passionate about sharing with others. Ask God to help you to be more faithful and bold in sharing this truth with your world.

transform your life through a journey of discovery into the world of the Bible

Faith Lessons Video Series

Filmed on location in Israel, **Faith Lessons** is a unique video series that brings God's Word to life with astounding relevance. By weaving together the Bible's fascinating historical, cultural, religious, and geographical contexts, teacher and historian Ray Vander Laan reveals keen insights into Scripture's significance for modern believers. These illuminating "faith lessons" afford a new understanding of the Bible that will ground your convictions and transform your life.

The **Faith Lessons** video series is ideal for use at home, especially in personal and family Bible studies. Individual believers and families will gain vital insights from long-ago times and cultures through this innovative approach to Bible study.

"Nothing has opened and illuminated the Scriptures for me quite like the Faith Lessons series."

—Dr. James Dobson

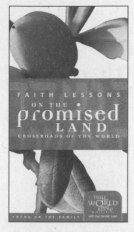

**Faith Lessons on
the Promised Land**
Crossroads of the World
**Volume One
0-310-67864-1**

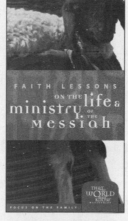

**Faith Lessons on
the Life & Ministry
of the Messiah
Volume Three
0-310-67866-8**

**Faith Lessons on
the Prophets &
Kings of Israel
Volume Two
0-310-67865-X**

**Faith Lessons on the
Death & Resurrection
of the Messiah
Volume Four
0-310-67867-6**

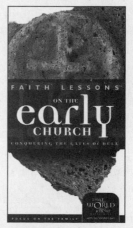

**Faith Lessons on
the Early Church
Volume Five
0-310-67962-1**

Travel back in time to see the sights, hear the sounds, and experience the wonder of Jesus—all through the power of interactive CD-ROM.

Jesus
An Interactive Journey

Imagine traveling back in time for a life-changing encounter with Christ . . . meeting the people who knew Him . . . retracing His footsteps . . . seeing first-hand what His life was like.

Now, through the cutting-edge technology of interactive CD-ROM, you can make that incredible voyage—back to the life and times of Jesus! This exciting multimedia adventure takes you there, giving you an entirely new appreciation for the fascinating historical, geographical, and cultural backdrop that will enhance your understanding of the Gospel.

An innovative "Visitor's Center" is your gateway to more than 180 different avenues of study, from Christ's birth to His resurrection. With a click of the mouse, you'll be guided to dozens of colorful locales, where you'll experience through the eyes and ears of ancient Jews and Romans what Christ's world was really like.

Or take a self-guided tour and stroll at your own pace through the lively marketplace to learn about trade and commerce, pause to listen in on the people, or go to the synagogue to gain a better understanding of the religious practices of the day.

Compatible with Windows® 95 and Windows® 3.1

0-310-67888-9